The Lazy Person's Guide to Success

OTHER NOTABLE BOOKS BY ERNIE J. ZELINSKI

How to Retire Happy, Wild, and Free: *Retirement Wisdom That You Won't Get from Your Financial Advisor* (Over 400,000 copies sold and published in 10 foreign languages)

The Joy of Not Working: *A Book for the Retired, Unemployed, and Overworked* (Over 310,000 copies sold and published in 17 foreign languages)

Career Success Without a Real Job: *The Career Book for People Too Smart to Work in Corporations*

Look Ma, Life's Easy: *How Ordinary People Attain Extraordinary Success and Remarkable Prosperity* (Published in 7 languages)

101 Really Important Things You Already Know, But Keep Forgetting: (Over 50,000 copies sold and published in 10 languages)

The Joy of Being Retired: *365 Reasons Why Retirement Rocks — and Work Sucks!*

Life's Secret Handbook: *Reminders for Adventurous Souls Who Want to Make a Big Difference in This World*

The Lazy Person's Guide to Success

Financial Independence and Personal Freedom Too!

Ernie J. Zelinski

Visions International Publishing

ISBN: 978-0-9813118-4-5 (Print Edition)
ISBN: 978-1-927452-06-6 (eBook Edition)

FOREIGN EDITIONS:
Published in Spanish by Ediciones B, Barcelona
Published in French for Europe by Groupe Eyrol, Paris
Published in French for Canada by Stanké International,
  Montreal
Published in Chinese traditional characters by Think Tank
  Publishing, Taipei
Published in Chinese simplified characters by CITIC
  Publishing House, Beijing
Published in Arabic by Dar El Farasha Publishing, Beirut
Published in Korean by Mulpure Publishing, Seoul
Published in Japanese in by Eiji Publishing, Tokyo
Published in Russian by Prime-Evroznak, St. Petersburg
Published in Portuguese by Editora Sextante, Rio de Janeiro
Published in Indonesian by PPM Publishing, Jakarta
Published in Dutch by Mirananda Uitgevers, The Hague
Published in Bulgarian by Kibea, Sophia
First published in English by Ten Speed Press, Berkeley, CA

Contents

Introduction 1

**Chapter 1: To Be More Successful, Try Working Less
and Thinking More** 11

Most Success Costs Too Much 13
The Conduct of Society Is a Poor Precedent for Living
   a Happy Life 21
The Most Creative Shortcut to Success is to Reevaluate
   What Success Means to You 29
Not Doing Anything for What You Want Is More Difficult
   than Working Hard for It 37
You Can't Always Get What You Want, but You Can Get
   a Lot More than Think You Can 45
Hard Work Is No Match for Relaxed, Creative Action 53
3C Vision Will Help Make You More Successful than
   3D Vision 57

**Chapter 2: Work at What You Are and Not at What
You Ain't** 63

Neither Wealth nor Splendor, but Tranquility and
   Occupation Give Happiness 65
It's Not What You Become, but What You Don't Become
   That Will Hurt Most in the End 77
Controlling Your Destiny Is More Important than the
   Size of Your Paycheck 85
Paying Your Dues Isn't Easy, but It's Easier than Not
   Paying Them 93
Selling Just a Bit of Your Soul for $10,000 Today Will
   Cost You Much More Later On 101

Chapter 3: Your Creativity Makes You a Millionaire 109

There's No Off-Switch on Your Genius Machine 111
The More Creative Your Thinking, the Fewer Your Cares
   and Worries 117
Security Is a Kind of Death 123
Opportunity Will Knock Often in the Future: How Often
   Will You Be Home? 129
Creative Loafing Is Good for Your Cash Flow 133

Chapter 4: Accept the Truth about Money and You Won't Have to Work So Hard **141**

Money Doesn't Talk; It Whispers 143
Money Solves All Problems — Except All Those That It
    Doesn't Solve 151
Financial Insanity Has Its Own Big Following — Including
    You and Me 157
Your Best Purchases Will Turn Out to Be the Ones That
    You Never Made 161
There's More to Life than Having It All 165

Chapter 5: You Have the Money, but Can You Buy Some Time? **171**

Being Successful at Work Is Irrelevant If You Are a
    Failure at Home 173
To Work Is Human, to Loaf Divine 179
Busyness Is the Last Refuge of Unproductive and
    Unfulfilled People 185
Most Things Worth Doing Aren't Worth Your Best Efforts . .195
All Things Worth Doing Well Aren't Worth Overdoing 199
Your Most Powerful Success Tool Is the 80-20 Rule 203
Slow Down and Your Days Will Be Longer 207

Chapter 6: The Journey toward Success Should Feel Better than the Arrival **213**

Only Fools Are in a Hurry to Get to Anywhere
    Worth Going 215
Life's a Breeze When We Put Half As Much Time into
    Simplifying It As We Do into Complicating It 219
Envy Is the Satisfaction and Happiness That We Think
    Others Are Experiencing 223
Be Happy While You Are Alive, Because You Are a Long
    Time Dead 227

INTRODUCTION

Let's face it: I have always been a lazy person. If my mother was alive today, she would agree. She would talk about how there were many chores to get done on the farm that we lived on for the first fourteen years of my life. My mother would ask my older brother to do chores and he would attend to them promptly. She would ask me the same and I would say, "Not now. I want to go for a bike ride. Maybe later." I would likely do some chores later, but only those that I liked and that I wanted to do. I haven't changed much over the years.

The first edition of this book was published in 2002 by Ten Speed Press but it went out of print in 2009. I always thought about putting it back in print knowing that it is a very good book. After all, it proved to be a true "international bestseller" by having sold over 110,000 copies and having been published in eleven languages. It just goes to show how "truly lazy" I can be with my taking ten years to get around to publishing a new edition. I did it because some readers say that this is the best book that I have ever written.

There is a little more of my true laziness related to this book. In 2001 I actually quit writing it after three chapters, doing the "Lazy" in the title proud. About two months later, a Spanish publisher asked me to send her some material relating to another one of my books. While I was packaging the material, on a whim I decided to include the three chapters from this book.

About two months later, I received an email from the publisher saying that she wanted to publish a Spanish edition. I had to think for awhile about this because I would only get a $3,000 US advance. I finally sent an email to the publisher accepting the advance and letting her know it would take me another three to six weeks to complete the other three chapters. She sent me an email back saying, "Oh, I thought the three chapters were the complete book."

As it turned out, there were five US publishers that wanted to publish this book in English. A few readers say that it's a really cool creative book given that the right pages have regular content whereas the left pages are "FOR THE TRULY LAZY" with a running summary of the content on the right pages.

FOR THE TRULY LAZY:

Anything great that has been accomplished in the history of humanity has started with one small thought.

We all have those thoughts.

Few people do anything with theirs, however.

What do you intend to do with yours?

More Wisdom for Being a Creative Lazy Achiever:

All that we are is the result of what we have thought.
— BUDDHA

Wealth is the product of man's capacity to think.
— AYN RAND

In every work of genius, we recognize our rejected thoughts.
— RALPH WALDO EMERSON

Now to the crux of the matter: Some advice just seems too good to be true. One such bit of advice is "Work hard and you will get what you want out of life." Indeed, nothing could be further from the truth. Many people in the Western world work long and hard for years and don't even come close to getting what they want out of life. Moreover, people in less-developed countries work even longer and harder but wind up with a lot less.

Clearly, there has never been so much wealth in industrialized countries. Yet magazines and papers today are full of articles about the increased stress and dissatisfaction present in Western society as a result of overwork. Any sane person should be saying, "What the heck is going on here? We must be crazy to conduct our lives in ways that are destroying our minds, bodies, and souls." Sadly, most individuals today are far too emotionally locked into work to realize how harmful it can be to themselves and others.

A major premise of this book is that hard work leads to inadequate results, not to mention frustration, fatigue, excess stress, and nervous twitching. Unfortunately, we have been conditioned to think that success must depend upon long hours, busyness, little leisure time, and other major sacrifices. The problem is that working ten or twelve hours a day leaves little time for real living — the activities that contribute to satisfaction and happiness.

In this age of busyness, most people are time-deprived to the point of exhaustion. Contrary to popular wisdom, it doesn't have to be this way. There is no shortage of time. People squander their time on insignificant activities and on the pursuit of goals that contribute nothing to success and happiness.

Today, money and material possessions — the symbols of happiness often take priority over lifestyle. Truth be known, not only are money and material possessions not happiness, the pursuit of these false symbols of happiness contributes to much unhappiness. As long as lifestyle is subordinated to money and material possessions, there will be little happiness. It should go without saying that people who lack happiness in their lives cannot consider themselves truly successful.

Although few people stop to think about it, there is an alternative to the work-until-you-drop mentality prevalent in much of western society today. The

FOR THE TRULY LAZY:

The fact is, most things in this world don't really matter.

It's a big mistake to pursue things that don't matter at the expense of the few things that do matter.

More Wisdom for Being a Creative Lazy Achiever:

It is not enough to be busy . . . . The question is: what are we busy about?

— HENRY DAVID THOREAU

If you burn the candle at both ends, you are not as bright as you think.

— UNKNOWN WISE PERSON

Hard work is simply hard work. It has nothing to do with the quality of your results and how much you will accomplish in life.

— LIFE'S SECRET HANDBOOK

alternative is to pursue only the things that make a difference in the quality of life. In fact, only a few things in life really do matter. The really important things affect success and happiness a great deal more than people realize. By the same token, the less important things contribute a lot less to success and happiness than people realize.

The road to unhappiness is paved with the pursuit of things that matter little. In fact, most pursuits are completely unnecessary and pointless. The goals of these pursuits include longer job titles, bigger houses, flashier cars, and trendier activities. After all is said and done, however, only a few things contribute significantly to achievement and happiness.

One reason people pursue the less important things is that practically everyone else in society is pursuing these things, which are really just status symbols. Yet following the norm is much more difficult — and a lot less worthwhile — than commonly thought. Most activity in which people indulge is just busyness, resulting in little meaningful achievement and in even less satisfaction. Worse, not only are many activities trivial, they can have a negative effect on intended results.

If you are like most people, you put way too much time into the wrong things and not enough time into the right ones. Working long and hard at the wrong things won't get you very far in life. Working a small amount on the right things can bring you success and well-being not experienced by 95 percent of humankind, however.

As hard as it may be for you to believe, you can work less and still earn more money and enjoy life much more. It's a basic matter of following the adage of working smart and not hard. Time devoted to hard work is generally poorly used time, whereas time given to creativity and imagination is the most effectively used time. Not only does hard work count little toward success, but the amount of each resource you have at your disposal also counts little. Clearly, it's how effectively you use what you have at your disposal that counts. The wise use of your assets — time, energy, creativity, motivation, money, patience, and courage — is what will bring you great success, financial independence, and personal freedom over the long term.

FOR THE TRULY LAZY:

What most people think is important for creative success is not so significant after all is said and done.

And what most people think is insignificant is vastly more important than most people could ever imagine.

So to be more successful, learn to distinguish between the truly unimportant and the truly important.

Eventually, you will be considered not only a genius, but a messiah as well.

More Wisdom for Being a Creative Lazy Achiever:

You will never reach your destination if you stop and throw stones at every dog that barks.
— *WINSTON CHURHILL*

Doing nothing is better than being busy doing nothing.
— *LAO TZU*

Someone once said that if you want something done faster and easier, give it to a lazy person. This book is about being that lazy person. Clearly, I am not talking about being lazy in a slothful, haphazard, and unproductive manner. Quite the opposite: I believe in productive laziness. Viewed this way, laziness can contribute a lot of value to your life.

In this book, the term Creative Lazy Achiever represents an individual who practices positive, productive laziness. The Creative Lazy Achiever will attain success with moderate effort. Indeed, using the Creative Lazy Achiever's principles is relatively easy compared to following "the work hard, play little" strategy of most people in western society today. Those who adopt these principles will realize this when they compare the rewards with the effort required to attain these rewards.

Although the Creative Lazy Achiever's principles are quite basic, I won't suggest that practicing them is easy. A measure of commitment and an adequate amount of sustained effort are required. The net result will be that your life is a lot easier than it would have been had you followed conventional wisdom in regards to what brings success.

To be sure, to be moderately lazy and highly productive, you have to be intelligent and creative. The key is to focus on important results, not on the number of hours put in, as is the focus of hardworking — and hardheaded individuals. The difference can be remarkable in terms of the income you make and the balanced lifestyle you are able to enjoy.

It should go without saying that you must be good at identifying what is important in your life and what isn't. What is important includes not only activities in which you are involved today, but also goals that you are pursuing. Perhaps what you are striving for isn't as important as you may think. In other words, your goals may be ones that, once attained, won't contribute anything to your happiness and well-being.

Once you are crystal clear about which things will bring you the most satisfaction, you must discover the most efficient ways of getting them. This entails identifying the important activities that will bring you the most results. Maximizing the time you spend doing what you love and the things you are

FOR THE TRULY LAZY:

One of the great creations of the human mind is a perception of reality that has absolutely no relationship to it.

So be careful with what you perceive as reality.

Any misinterpretation of it is a lie.

This will cause you all sorts of big problems in life.

You are liable to wind up a bystander in an exciting and happening world.

More Wisdom for Being a Creative Lazy Achiever:

Have you ever considered that your perception of reality could be wrong? If you haven't, this is a sure sign that it is!

— LIFE'S SECRET HANDBOOK

good at will also help you attain what you want in life. By the same token, you must minimize the time you spend on things that you don't like and on things that you aren't good at.

Some of the fundamentals in this book may appear to be ones that should be obvious to any rational human being. Agreed: the principles are nothing more than common sense. This can be a hindrance to adopting them, however. For some strange reason, human beings choose to ignore anything obvious or anything that speaks of common sense. Perhaps most individuals on some level like to complicate things to add more dimensions to their lives. This makes them feel more important.

In the event that you yourself don't have some underlying perverse need to complicate your life, then the Creative Lazy Achiever's principles are for you. Not only will these principles help you attain more success, they will help you attain freedom not experienced by most people in the western world. Pay particular attention to these words of wisdom by one of my favorite writers: **"It's better to do a subpar job on the right project than an excellent job on the wrong project."** These important words by Robert J. Ringer have helped me attain the great prosperity and personal freedom that I enjoy today — and are the foundation of this book.

You can read this book in three ways. First is to read both the right and left pages. The material on the left pages represents the topic areas on the right pages, but in different words and more to the point. Some people may find the left pages a little more poetic as well. Second is to focus only on the left pages. In the event you are time-deprived, this method will allow you to get the whole drift of the book in a fraction of the time required to read the whole book. Third is to read the left pages as a summary after you have read the entire book.

Irrespective of which method you choose for reading, this book shows you how to be successful — on your own terms. The Creative Lazy Achiever's principles are applicable at your workplace, in your home, and anywhere else you choose to use them. Dare to follow these principles, and you can become more creative, more insightful, more productive, more playful, wealthier, and happier — all by working less and enjoying life more.

FOR THE TRULY LAZY:

Speaking of reality, have you ever considered that hard work is not all it is cracked up to be?

Well, you should.

Accepting this will change your life.

More Wisdom for Being a Creative Lazy Achiever:

There is no kind of idleness by which we are so easily seduced as that which dignifies itself by the appearance of business.
— SAMUEL JOHNSON

You'll never succeed in idealizing hard work. Before you can dig mother earth you've got to take off your ideal jacket. The harder a man works at brute labor, the thinner becomes his idealism, the darker his mind.
— D. H. LAWRENCE

Chapter 1

To Be More Successful, Try

WORKING LESS

and

THINKING MORE

FOR THE TRULY LAZY:

Here's some more reality for you to think carefully about:

In Western society, the most important factor keeping many people from being successful is that they don't work hard enough.

For even more people, however, the most important factor keeping them from true success is that they work much too hard.

More Wisdom for Being a Creative Lazy Achiever:

It doesn't matter how fast or how hard you work if your efforts don't create value for others.
— *ROBERT J. RINGER*

The wisdom of a learned man cometh by opportunity of leisure: and he that hath little business shall become wise.
— *APOCRYPHA, ECCLESIASTICUS 38:25*

MOST SUCCESS COSTS TOO MUCH

Here's a favorite story to get you tuned up for the rest of this book. I often share it with happy, leisurely individuals when they tell me that they might have become millionaires if only they had worked a lot harder. The story helps them put life back in proper perspective. It may help you do the same.

A wealthy entrepreneur from New York went on a two-week seaside holiday on the coast of Costa Rica. On his first day there, he was impressed with the quality and taste of the exotic fish he bought from a local fisherman. The next day, the American encountered the native Costa Rican at the dock, but the Costa Rican had already sold his catch. The American discovered that the fisherman had a secret fishing spot where the fish were plenty and the quality superb. He only caught five or six fish each day, however.

The New Yorker asked the local fisherman why he didn't stay out longer at sea and catch more fish.

"But Senor," the fisherman replied, "I sleep in late until nine or ten every morning; I play with my children; I go fishing for an hour or two; in the afternoon I take a one- or two-hour siesta; in the early evening I have a relaxing meal with my family; and later in the evening, I go to the village and drink wine, play guitar, and sing with my amigos. As you can see, I have a full, relaxed, satisfying, and happy life."

The New Yorker replied, "You should catch a lot more fish. That way you could prepare for a prosperous future. Look, I am a businessman from New York, and I can help you become a lot more successful in life. I received an MBA from Harvard, and I know a lot about business and marketing."

The New Yorker continued. "The way to prepare for the future is to get up early in the morning and spend the whole day fishing, even going back for more in the evening. In no time, with the extra money, you could buy a bigger boat. Two years from now, you could have five or six boats that you could rent to other fishermen. In another five years, with all the fish you will control, you can build a fish plant and even have your own brand of fish products.

FOR THE TRULY LAZY:

R eality says that water is wet.

R ocks are hard.

Y ou have what it takes to be successful.

A nd you don't have to work hard at it.

More Wisdom for Being a Creative Lazy Achiever:

How to succeed: try hard enough. How to fail: try too hard.
— MALCOLM FORBES

Your creativity allows an idea to manifest itself. Your actions allow the idea to become real and start a life of its own. Your commitment to the idea allows it to eventually come to its natural perfect end as an important benefit to both you and the rest of humanity.
— LIFE'S SECRET HANDBOOK

"Then, in another six or seven years," the New Yorker continued, while the Costa Rican looked more and more bewildered, "you could leave here and move to New York or San Francisco and have someone else run your factory while you market your products. If you work hard for fifteen or twenty years, you could become a multimillionaire. Then you wouldn't have to work another day for the rest of your life."

"What would I do then, Senor?" responded the fisherman.

Without any hesitation, the wealthy New York businessman enthusiastically replied, "Then you would be able to move to a little village in some laid-back country like Mexico where you could sleep in late every day, play with the village children, take a long siesta every afternoon, eat meals while relaxing in the evening, and play guitar, sing, and drink wine with your amigos every night."

The moral of this story is that most success, as Western society defines it today, costs too much in terms of physical and mental health, family and social life, and personal freedoms. What's the point of working hard for many years, sacrificing happiness and well-being along the way, when you can have happiness and well-being today by not working so hard?

Fame and fortune may be on your list of life's rewards; the price you will have to pay for them in terms of time, energy, personal sacrifices, and risk may be higher than you care to expend, however. Of course, anything worth having always has a price, as is stressed later in this book — but some things aren't worth having for the high price attached to them. Oddly enough, the people in less-developed countries tend to know this better than many people in the more industrialized nations.

Frequently, we give little thought to the price some people pay in their pursuit of success. For many years, *Success* magazine featured people who had succeeded as entrepreneurs. More often than not, the magazine made the financial accomplishments of these individuals appear relatively easy. All told, most of these entrepreneurs had paid a big price for their success in terms of long work hours, little family life, risk to the family fortune, and emotional and physical suffering. *Success* magazine, however, didn't give much attention to the sacrifices that successful women and men had to make over many years.

FOR THE TRULY LAZY:

Zen masters stress the importance of being fully conscious of who we are and what we are doing.

Indeed, Buddha means "An Awakened One."

So being awake means to be attentive to the choices you make in the activities you pursue.

Clearly, working hard at the wrong things, even if you do them very well, won't get you much success and happiness in life.

More Wisdom for Being a Creative Lazy Achiever:

Nothing is often a good thing to do, and almost a good thing to say.
— WILL DURANT

I know of nothing more despicable and pathetic than a man who devotes all the hours of the waking day to the making of money for money's sake.
— JOHN D. ROCKEFELLER

Sadly, few people achieve success worthy of media exposure, regardless of how hard they work. Most jump into business ventures and high-status careers for the sole purpose of making money, or attaining power and fame, with little consideration to their skills, talents, and passions. The lack of joy and satisfaction in their pursuits dramatically increases their chances for eventual disappointment and failure.

Tens of thousands of people are at this very moment striving to be millionaires but will never reach their goal. They will toil long and hard in their basements for years developing products, devising business plans, and attempting to attract venture capital for their startups, before finally going broke. Undoubtedly, the success rate for these wannabe millionaires would be much higher if they would pursue business ventures more in tune with their own personal natures and passions instead of solely for the monetary potential.

Many pursuits that initially appeal to us can be counterproductive beyond measure in the long term. If you work hard enough, you may eventually attain riches — even fame — but always with a price. The question is, Are you willing to pay the price? It's always easy to say yes without having a full appreciation of the dilemmas and circumstances that you may have to face.

In your search for fame and fortune, the price may be a lot larger than you can ever imagine. You may have to sacrifice pleasures and luxuries while you dedicate your time, money, and energy in your moneymaking ventures. Creative pursuits, social activities, and family outings fall by the wayside when making money becomes the main objective in life. Besides, as you pursue this goal, you will be a poor marriage partner and a lousy parent. The temptation to get rich may even influence you to compromise your values and integrity.

Are you prepared to pay any of the aforementioned prices? Indeed, there are many more costs as well. What about the costs of health, freedom, and self-respect? These are short-term prices, relatively speaking. There is a longterm price that may be even more costly. Working eighteen hours a day, while others work seven or eight, may be a huge price to pay for something that cannot provide the happiness you ultimately expect. Trust me, this happens to a lot more people than one would expect.

FOR THE TRULY LAZY:

Never feel guilty about being lazy.

Society wants you to believe that being lazy is being unproductive.

On the contrary:

Being lazy is minimizing the time spent on things you don't like doing and maximizing the time spent on things you enjoy doing.

More Wisdom for Being a Creative Lazy Achiever:

The man who does not betake himself at once and desperately to sawing is called a loafer, though he may be knocking at the doors of heaven all the while.
— *HENRY DAVID THOREAU*

Instead of expending time to train yourself not to be afraid of snakes, avoid them altogether.
— *RICHARD KOCH*

It may surprise you, or even pain you, to find out that many people, after having attained fame and fortune, regret having devoted all their life energy to getting there. I am not talking about neurotic, confused individuals who don't have a clue about what they want in life. I am talking about intelligent, well-balanced, accomplished, highly respected individuals in mainstream society.

Take, for example, George Soros, the famous currency speculator. Using his financial savvy, Soros amassed a fortune that has been estimated at $5 billion. Yet he claims that he would trade it all for a chance to have achieved his career dream. The intellectual pursuit — not the making of money — has always been his real passion.

Recently, Soros told a reporter for Canada's *National Post* newspaper, "It would give me a great deal more satisfaction if I was recognized as a philosopher." Asked by the reporter if he would give all his money away for that, he replied, "Well, yes definitely."

The experience of George Soros is not uncommon. Thousands of people have worked hard, accumulated a substantial amount of money, and concluded that it wasn't worth it. They realized that with less money, they would only have given up things they didn't need anyway. Moreover, they realized that they would have enjoyed themselves more along the way had they worked less.

Some things worth having cannot be measured in dollars and cents. One is a full, relaxed, happy, and satisfying life today. Sacrificing a relaxed lifestyle today for a possible equivalent with more money sometime in the far distant future seems asinine indeed. Such sacrifice certainly doesn't contribute to present-day happiness and prosperity consciousness.

The alternative to working long and hard for many years, while sacrificing present-day happiness, is being satisfied and content today. Be happy in the present moment, in other words, as advocated by Eckhart Tolle in his blockbuster book *The Power of Now*. Work at something that you enjoy, and at the same time, spend plenty of time on constructive leisure activities. This requires that you be a somewhat lazy but highly prolific individual.

FOR THE TRULY LAZY:

M ost people go to their graves regretting things they haven't done.

T he easiest way to become one of them is by joining society's chorus instead of singing your own songs.

More Wisdom for Being a Creative Lazy Achiever:

When all think alike, then no one is thinking.
— WALTER LIPPMANN

Most well-trodden paths lead nowhere.
— UNKNOWN WISE PERSON

You want to be known for your spirit, your creativity, and the difference you make in this world. To be nimble-witted, spiritually aware, and street-smart is to be abreast of the advanced and magical workings of the Universe.
— LIFE'S SECRET HANDBOOK

THE CONDUCT OF SOCIETY IS A POOR PRECEDENT FOR LIVING A HAPPY LIFE

In 1919, when criticized for continually arriving late for work, Lord Castlerousse retorted, "But think how early I go." Now I don't know about you, but I like this guy's attitude. Going to work late and leaving early prevented Lord Castlerousse from becoming an unhappy Workaholic. Undoubtedly, he enjoyed more free time than most workers of his era. Clearly, he knew how to live a better-balanced lifestyle than most people do today.

This leads us into a major problem in contemporary society: most people don't know how to truly live and enjoy themselves in the present. Adopting a more relaxed and carefree attitude, as displayed by Lord Castlerousse, would do wonders for the overall well-being of these people.

By the time the twenty-first century began in earnest, the economy in most Western nations had been roaring along for many years — like never before, in fact. Yet regular media reports indicated that many workers, including well-paid professionals and executives, were experiencing low morale, burnout, and a diminished quality of life. Indeed, every year brought another new study concluding that people were more stressed out and less satisfied than they had been the year before.

For a few years the economic conditions took a turn for the worse and the situation was the same as it was in good times. Now that we are into good times again, ask most hardworking Americans how things are going for them, and you will hear stories of sixty- to seventy-hour weeks, with no time for rest. The result is not only physical exhaustion, but also emotional burnout, contributing to experiences of hopelessness and quiet desperation.

Among the many telling signs of this sad situation is that individuals lack substance in their everyday living. People are leading anything but full, relaxed, satisfying, and happy lives. Being successful in the twenty-first century means having more work and less time to do the things one would like. To be sure, many of the most successful people in Europe and the Americas

FOR THE TRULY LAZY:

Always question what your neighbors say or do or think.

It's unwise to use the conduct of the majority in society as a viable precedent for your own life.

Do so and you will be setting yourself up for much disappointment and disillusionment.

What the majority pursues is seldom what will bring happiness, satisfaction, and freedom to any individual's life.

More Wisdom for Being a Creative Lazy Achiever:

He who joyfully marches in rank and file has already earned my contempt. He has been given a large brain by mistake, since for him the spinal cord would have been enough.
— ALBERT EINSTEIN

Any fool can run toward the light. It takes a Master with courage to turn and face the darkness and shine his own light there.
— LESLIE FIEGLER

today are dissatisfied with themselves and with their lives in general. Some of these won't-ever-make-it workaholics may even be envying the dead like Dilbert in Scott Adam's cartoon of the same name.

Moreover, despite having had their incomes far outpace their real needs, middle- and upper-middle-class individuals, especially in Canada and the United States, are indulging in an uncontrollable national binge of spending and living beyond their means. To keep themselves out of bankruptcy court, they must continue working in jobs that leave them frustrated and unfulfilled. They work an outrageous number of hours; consequently, they spend little time with friends and family. If they do manage to find some free time, these people are too far in debt, too unhappy, too tired, and too miserable to enjoy any of it.

Even the most affluent people are trapped by lifestyles that economic prosperity has provided. They are making a great living but living a lousy life. Walk through any ritzy neighborhood and see how many people are enjoying themselves on their front porches of their classy homes. Most affluent people have neither the time to enjoy themselves nor the ability to enjoy themselves even if they did have some spare time. Like poorly paid workers, high-income earners keep on striving for more wealth and success but never seem to get closer to peace of mind and happiness.

Most individuals are in a state of unconsciousness or self-denial about how their lives are out of sync with their deepest values and beliefs. They miss more children's birthdays, anniversaries, and other family functions than they will ever admit.

The way I see it, the biggest contributor to this pitiful situation is people's willingness to go along with what everyone else is doing. The herd instinct is powerful indeed, perhaps because it doesn't require that people think on their own. Sadly, the majority of people allow others to take control of their lives.

Erich Fromm in *Escape from Freedom* wrote, "Modern man lives under the illusion that he knows what he wants, while he actually wants what he is supposed to want." For sure, in today's consumer society, advertisers and the media dictate what people are supposed to want. Many people consume this programming greedily instead of stopping to question what will truly make

FOR THE TRULY LAZY:

You will have a much easier go-around in life when you stop following the herd.

Your chances for a full, relaxed, satisfying, and happy life will tend to increase in direct proportion to how much you are out of step with the rest of society.

Indeed, the more unconventional and eccentric you are, the better.

More Wisdom for Being a Creative Lazy Achiever:

That so few now dare to be eccentric, marks the chief danger of the time.
— *JOHN STUART MILL*

If you see in any given situation only what everybody else can see, you can be said to be so much a representative of your culture that you are a victim of it.
— *S. I. HAYAKAWA*

them happy. After all, it's much easier to try to fit in with the majority than to question what the majority is doing and then do something different.

When it comes to having a successful life, as defined in western society today, the two options seem to be (1) staying within the system and working long and hard hours, or (2) dropping out of the system completely to pursue a life of total leisure. To be sure, for most people, this is a choice between two zeroes. On one hand, people don't want to work longer and harder; on the other, they haven't attained the financial independence to drop out completely.

How do you fit into this picture? Perhaps you are like most people who have a good living in economic terms. You probably make a decent income that allows you to provide much more than life's necessities. Working long and hard just for security, status, power, and possessions leaves a lot to be desired, however. Something spiritual and psychological may be missing. Undoubtedly, if your work and life are in horrible balance, you don't create the time required to pursue the productive leisure activities that can satisfy your emotional and spiritual needs.

Perhaps this statement will excite indignation from you, as do most statements that are true but that you want to deny: if your life is far from being as satisfying and fulfilling as you would like it to be, you have created this mess in the first place. Ultimately, no one is forcing you to lead a hurried life; you alone have chosen to do so. This makes you totally responsible for any physical stress and emotional turmoil you bring into your life. And it stems from your willingness to go along with what everyone else is doing.

You may take comfort in knowing that you are in the large majority of individuals whose lives are chaotic and unbalanced. It may appear easier to follow the herd than to think differently and do things on your own. You will always follow the herd at your peril, however. The problem with herds is that they occasionally start stampedes that are hard to stop. And when a herd causes a lot of damage, none of its members is willing to take responsibility.

Far too few people in this world think for themselves. Instead of allowing their own creativity and inner wisdom to run their lives, they prefer what others are doing and thinking. You don't have to be one of those people. As an active,

FOR THE TRULY LAZY:

For Creative Lazy Achievers, one of the keys to success is refusing to accept society's definition of success as their own.

It's wise to define success on your own terms and not on someone else's.

By doing this, you will attain success in a much more relaxed and satisfying manner.

More Wisdom for Being a Creative Lazy Achiever:

What the crowd requires is mediocrity of the highest order.
— ANTOINE-AUGUSTE PREAULT

It is cruel to discover one's mediocrity only when it is too late.
— W. SOMERSET MAUGHAM

The only way to win and be successful, sometimes — is just to be happy and blown away with what you already have today.
— LIFE'S SECRET HANDBOOK

creative, thinking human being, you should realize that — contrary to popular wisdom — you always have an alternative to following the herd. While the herd is moving in one direction, in fact, you can go in any of several other directions. That's what I do because I have my own way to rock.

Following the majority as they look for happiness in all the wrong places is pointless. Why waste time, energy, and money chasing after something that you don't really need and may not even enjoy? Some things are important, and others are not. Some things appear to be important because people have been brainwashed by society, educational institutions, and advertisers to believe that they are important. Upon close scrutiny, most of these things have no relevance whatsoever to leading a happy and healthy lifestyle.

The more attention you pay to what the masses are doing, the more you will realize that the everybody-else-is-doing-it approach isn't the way to put your mark on this world. While it's tempting to join the masses, always remember that you have more meaningful dreams and more important things to pursue.

One of your most important goals in life should be to be you and not anyone else. When Leonardo da Vinci was asked what his greatest accomplishment had been in his life, he replied, "Leonardo da Vinci." In this regard, Zen masters don't ask us to be something or someone we aren't; instead, they ask us to be more truly and more fully who we are.

Probably the hardest thing about living a satisfying and prosperous life is to be true to our own fancies and refrain from going along with the masses. At the best of times, chasing after the approval of others by emulating them is a zero-results game. To be impressed by others and their possessions is to lose your true self.

Being truly and fully who you are requires knowing what's important to you, and only to you. You have to make sure that your life's choices are your own. This was best said by American poet, painter, and playwright e. e. cummings, "To be nobody — but yourself — in a world which is doing its best, night and day, to make you like everybody else — means to fight the hardest battle any human being can fight; and never stop fighting."

FOR THE TRULY LAZY:

If you want more success and happiness, answer these two questions:

What is success?

And what is happiness?

You may not have to do anything more than to keep asking these questions to bring more joy, satisfaction, and contentment into your life.

More Wisdom for Being a Creative Lazy Achiever:

If your success is not achieved according to your ideals, if your success is impressive to society but does not resonate with your psyche and spirit, then it is not true success at all.
— LIFE'S SECRET HANDBOOK

You have reached the pinnacle of success as soon as you become uninterested in money, compliments, or publicity.
— DR. O. A. BATTISTA

THE MOST CREATIVE SHORTCUT TO SUCCESS IS TO REEVALUATE WHAT SUCCESS MEANS TO YOU

This is one of the most important points made in this book: For more success in your life, try working less but thinking more than the average person in society does. The degree to which you develop your ability to think differently and creatively will determine how successful you become and how hard you will have to work to attain your success.

The first question requiring a great deal of deep thought is, What does success actually mean to you? What success is, of course, varies from person to person. Two people can have accomplished similar things in their lives. Yet those who are optimists will see themselves as successful, whereas those who are pessimists will see themselves as failures. Moreover, a particular individual will see success differently at different times.

The hardest way to achieve success is to have someone else define it for you. Listen to friends, relatives, society, the media, and advertisers, and you are headed for big trouble. You will end up feeling a lot of pressure to do it all — have an extremely attractive mate; raise a perfect family; have a well-paid job; take exotic vacations; live in a stately mansion; drive an overpriced, flashy car; and still save a million for retirement. Attaining all of these things may be possible, but it is highly improbable. Furthermore, even attaining all of these things can leave you feeling unsuccessful if these are not the things that you truly want out of life.

As a rational human being, you should always be alert to creative shortcuts to success. In this regard, the most creative shortcut to success is to think more about what success means to you. Ultimately, you will make yourself successful or unsuccessful just by the way you define success.

Undoubtedly, the most serious mistake people make is failing to define success in the most personal way. I know what success means to me. How about you? Can you specifically identify how your definition of success is different from the conventional definition involving fame and fortune?

FOR THE TRULY LAZY:

When you contemplate what true success really is, you may be too frightened to see the answer.

You may have to shatter the dream that you have built.

You will always remain discontented and unfulfilled when your primary goal is conventional success.

More Wisdom for Being a Creative Lazy Achiever:

Some aspects of success seem rather silly as death approaches.
— DONALD A. MILLER

Find out what you like doing best and get someone to pay you for it.
— KATHARINE WHITEHORN

The three most harmful addictions are heroin, carbohydrates, and a monthly salary.
— FRED WILSON

Of course, you must be reasonable in the amount of success you hope to achieve. A big obstacle to attaining success is to expect too much. Setting reasonable goals makes the attainment of success much easier. On the other hand, you don't want to go too far on the easy side. Your goal shouldn't be to have everything be easy. Attaining such a goal would leave you without a sense of achievement and with little satisfaction.

Happiness and satisfaction will only come when you achieve something of importance. Effort and risk must be involved in attaining results to bring a sense of true achievement. The key is to choose goals big enough to make a difference and modest enough to be attained. Ultimately, it is probably better to set moderately difficult goals and to achieve most of them than to set extremely difficult goals and not to achieve any of them.

With Zenlike attention to detail, it's best to take a holistic approach when defining what success means to you. Success should constitute all the things that will make you happy in life. These include meaningful work; mental, physical, and spiritual health; friendship; love; security; peace of mind; and plenty of free time.

Out of curiosity, you may wonder what success means to me. Although my definition of success may change with time, it doesn't vary much. Success to me is having the freedom and independence to make choices in what I do with my life. It means doing what I want at the time I choose.

After I get up around noon, my first priorities are to exercise one to two hours to maintain my health and to pursue other leisure activities such as meeting friends at a coffee bar. Unlike the majority of people, I fit my work in whenever I can, usually writing on my laptop in one of my favorite coffee bars. Most days I end up working only four or five hours, sometimes much less. Occasionally I work seven or eight hours.

Although I don't make as much money as I could by working an hour or two more each day, I live comfortably and freely. I certainly wouldn't trade my present lifestyle for a stressful job that paid ten million dollars a year, not even for one year. This was also the case many years ago when I was struggling financially, $30,000 in debt and sometimes not knowing where my next

FOR THE TRULY LAZY:

The one thing that can be more disappointing than failure is success itself, because success doesn't always bring us what we thought it would.

To have achieved the success that you have always dreamed about can seem quite silly once you have attained it especially if you have dedicated most of your life to being successful at the expense of life itself.

More Wisdom for Being a Creative Lazy Achiever:

People seldom see the halting and painful steps by which the most insignificant success is achieved.
— ANNE SULLIVAN

The best thing that comes with success is the knowledge that it is nothing to long for.
— LIV ULLMAN

month's rent was going to come from. Success to me is not being worth ten or twenty million dollars, although I would probably get satisfaction from attaining this status through my creative efforts.

In financial terms, true success to me is handling money wisely so that I don't have financial problems. It means earning the money to buy the necessities of life and having a little extra to pay for some luxuries, such as a meal at a great restaurant two or three times a week. Financial success is also the sense of freedom that comes from having saved a nice little nest egg. This can come in handy in the event I want to do nothing but play for a year or if my income drops for some reason.

Success to me is having not only the time, but the ability to enjoy leisure activities a lot. Many billionaires and multimillionaires may have the money to play at the most expensive games, but they don't have the ability to take it easy and enjoy the activities that don't cost any money. The way I see it, billionaires who don't have time to stop and talk to a street person for five minutes — to see what makes the street person tick — are missing out on a lot in life.

Put another way, these billionaires aren't that successful if they are ruled by money and work while being deprived of time to enjoy the small things in life. Indeed, if they can't enjoy simple activities, they probably don't get that much enjoyment out of the most expensive activities that money can buy.

Success to me is much more than plenty of leisure time. It is also the wise use of leisure time. Maintaining optimum health at any age must be a priority. This can be achieved only by allocating some leisure time for adequate exercise and meditation every day.

Above all, success is having a worthwhile purpose to pursue. My purpose is to help people develop their potential and make leisurely progress toward attaining some of their dreams. Like many authors, I receive feedback from readers. There is great satisfaction from receiving a handwritten letter, email, or phone call from someone who has benefited greatly from reading my books.

Another ingredient of success is having my own attainable dreams, regardless of how old I get. One of my dreams is to have one of my books appear on the *New York Times* best-seller list. Although achieving this goal is

FOR THE TRULY LAZY:

It's all too easy to get too intoxicated with the dream of what conventional success is going to do for our happiness.

Yet conventional success and happiness are two entirely different things.

Conventional success — a big house, a beach cabin, two or three fancy cars, an extremely attractive spouse, and a high-powered job — hardly serves any purpose other than to make life extremely difficult for most people.

More Wisdom for Being a Creative Lazy Achiever:

There is only one success . . . to be able to spend your life in your own way, and not to give others absurd maddening claims upon it.
— CHRISTOPHER MORLEY

Success is doing what you like and making a living at it.
— GREEK PROVERB

not essential to my happiness, I would get great satisfaction from doing so. This is one of my life's goals that keeps me motivated and brings me many smaller career successes along the way.

That's more than enough about what success means to me. Now back to you. Again, the big question is, What does success really mean to you? The degree to which you scale down your expectations of what a successful life should provide will determine how successful you feel. At the same time, you don't want to set your sights so low that you deprive yourself the satisfaction of achieving meaningful goals.

Being true to yourself is important. Upon close examination of your life, you may determine that some of the things you presently want — things that you are pursuing with great zeal — may be a lot less important to your happiness than you thought. On the other hand, some of the things that you are presently neglecting may be essential to your peace and contentment. If you want your life to change for the better, you may need to change your relationships with money, material possessions, time, work, leisure activities, and even people.

The defining moment for your success won't be when you have become a multimillionaire. In fact, the defining moment will be when you realize that you can't be any happier regardless of how much more money you have to your name. Some people are able to reach this state with a net value of under $100,000. Others never reach this state, despite having acquired millions.

Ultimately, living a successful life requires that you be in control of your mind. To be sure, you are definitely not in control of your mind if friends, relatives, society, the media, and advertisers strongly influence your view of true success. It thus behooves you to spend some significant time regularly evaluating and reevaluating what success means to you-and only to you.

The surest sign that you are on the right track to leading a full, relaxed, satisfying, and happy life is that you have clearly defined success in a way that is different than the definition of any other individual on Earth. Indeed, the most important definition of success — and whether you have attained that success — will always be in the eye of the beholder.

FOR THE TRULY LAZY:

In modern life, as in Greek tragedies, should we be astonished that many successful people aren't happy people?

In case you haven't noticed, conventional success is much easier to attain than is happiness.

There are tens of thousands of successful neurotics.

But there are no happy ones.

More Wisdom for Being a Creative Lazy Achiever:

Nothing recedes like success.
— BRYAN FORBES

The secret of success in life is known only to those who have not succeeded.
— JOHN CHURTON COLLINS

NOT DOING ANYTHING FOR WHAT YOU WANT IS MORE DIFFICULT THAN WORKING HARD FOR IT

The million-dollar question was, What does success mean to you? Now the two-million-dollar question is, How are you going to achieve it? This book is about how to be more successful by thinking more and working less than does the average person in society. It does not advocate a do-nothing approach that some people are looking for, however.

If you want to upgrade from the dump you're living in today to something closer to the Taj Mahal in the next few years, you will have to make some changes in your life. You will have to take a hard look at many things, such as the quality of your friends, how much TV you watch, how much time you spend on Facebook, your motivation level, how creative you are, your beliefs, your chosen career, your passions, and whether you suffer from the world-owes-me-a-living syndrome. To some degree, you will need to make some effort either to work more, change your line of work, or work smarter.

To make leisurely progress toward your dreams still takes courage and action. Even the fisherman in Costa Rica, who leads a full, relaxed, satisfying, and happy life, has to do something for it. He may work only a few hours a day, but he has to work enough to earn his keep. You must do the same if you want satisfaction and happiness to prevail in your life.

Some people prefer to get what they want without doing anything for it. Attaining success in this way is next to impossible, of course. Such a method for attaining success is infinitely difficult rather than easy. Doing nothing for what you want is thus more difficult than working hard for it.

Perhaps, like a lot of us, you tend to fall into the trap of believing that someone else will handle the challenging areas of your life, including paying for your way in this world. You may even feel justified in expecting someone else to provide you with a comfortable living and the personal freedom to do what you want. Being no opponent to your comfort and happiness, I will concede that, compared to me, you probably deserve it.

FOR THE TRULY LAZY:

To attain true success, we must clarify what we want in life.

The biggest problem isn't so much that we can't get what we think we want.

The biggest problem is that when we get what we think we want, it isn't what we want.

Indeed, what will keep us from getting what we truly want is not knowing exactly what that is.

More Wisdom for Being a Creative Lazy Achiever:

Take care to get what you like or you will be forced to like what you don't like.

— GEORGE BERNARD SHAW

Success for some people depends on becoming well-known, for others it depends on never being found out.

— ASHLEIGH BRILLIANT

Problem is, no one is likely to provide you and seven billion others who desire it — and think they deserve it — a comfortable living. Even if it were possible to attain some of the things we want without effort, this could not be considered success. To feel successful, we must experience a sense of achievement and feel that we deserve the things we have acquired.

This is not complicated. The best way to get what you want is to do something worthwhile for it. You can try working long and hard for it. Alternatively, you can be more creative and work a lot less so that you have more time to appreciate what you have attained. Either way, you will experience satisfaction from having attained what you want out of life. The second way allows you to enjoy life more, however.

In simple terms, the object is to get some of the things you want in life without experiencing undue stress and anxiety. Choose a reasonable amount of time you would like to work. It can be eight hours a day, or it can be as little as two or three. Then ensure that you give your best within that time frame — no more and no less.

I do not choose to work for more than five hours a day; however, I am intense when I do work on the right projects. I always try to do my best. To date, my first fifteen manuscripts have been published by at least one reputable foreign publisher. Yet book experts estimate that only one out of ten manuscripts published in North America gets published by a foreign publisher.

How do I attain my success rate of 100 percent while writers as a whole attain 10 percent? I simply do what has to be done. Fourteen of my books were originally rejected by English publishers; therefore, I self-published them first to prove their worth in the marketplace. The foreign publishers came next.

In fact, my signature best-selling book, *The Joy of Not Working*, was originally self-published in 1991, because no publisher was willing to publish it. I even had to borrow half of the money from my mother to do this, because I had only $5,000 in the bank and was still $30,000 in debt at that time. Since then, it has been published not only by Ten Speed Press in the United States, but also by seventeen other foreign publishers. The book has now sold over 310,000 copies worldwide. It goes without saying that this gives me a great

FOR THE TRULY LAZY:

It's just as hard to attain success through goals we don't have as it is to get pleasure from reminiscing about things we haven't done.

Thus, be clear about the type of success you would like and how you are going to get there.

More Wisdom for Being a Creative Lazy Achiever:

A thought which does not result in an action is nothing much, and an action which does not proceed from a thought is nothing at all.
— *GEORGES BERNANOS*

There exists above the "productive" man a yet higher species.
— *FRIEDRICH NIETZSCHE*

Getting results does not take time; it's the not getting results that takes all your time.
— *JOE POLISH*

sense of accomplishment. This would not have been possible if I had not put in my best effort in the four or five hours that I work each day.

To experience similar success in any field of endeavor, you must also do your personal best. There is nothing wrong with taking a more relaxed approach to earning a living. In fact, peak performers strive for a healthy balance between work and play. They know that there is more to life than continually working long and hard hours. Being on the other extreme is not the answer either, however. Devoting all of your time to nebulous activities leaves no time for the constructive, creative activities that are so extremely important for producing positive results.

"But I want some specific ways on how to earn exactly $750,000 in the next five years so I can retire and live in style and comfort for the rest of my life" is a common response. Sorry: the world doesn't work that way. If it's important to you, no one will do it for you. You must create a specific plan and corresponding strategy to get what you want out of life. Millions of other people can do it on their own; I can do it on my own; and so can you.

Getting what you want may not be easy, but plenty of help is available to accomplish anything you want. In books alone is a vast reserve of knowledge that can be exploited by anyone. Every answer to any problem you can ever imagine is in publication somewhere; you just need to find it. When I first started in this business, for example, I didn't have the faintest idea about how to get a book published. Everything I needed to know — the art of writing, how to self-publish, how to sell foreign rights, and creative ways to promote books — I was able to learn by reading books.

An incredible amount of information is available to you as well, regardless of what you want to accomplish. Besides using books, you can utilize other excellent resources such as consultants, seminars, radio talk shows, and all the great blogs and articles by experts on the Internet. Other people have acquired a lot of knowledge and wisdom that they make available either for free or at relatively low cost. Not only is the information a bargain, but your life will be a lot easier if you use it than if you had to go out and make the same mistakes these people have had to make.

FOR THE TRULY LAZY:

Determine your direction clearly before choosing the speed at which you want to travel.

In Western society, most people today are in a hurry to get to places not worth going.

Speed in life doesn't count as much as direction.

Indeed, where there is no direction, speed doesn't count at all.

More Wisdom for Being a Creative Lazy Achiever:

Never confuse movement with action.
— ERNEST HEMINGWAY

Ask yourself the secret to your success. Listen to your answer, and practice it.
— RICHARD BACH

To be sure, the road to success will have many obstacles. And there will be work, even if it's only four or five hours a day. Although Creative Lazy Achievers adopt a relaxed way to achieve prosperity and financial freedom, they also know that sustained effort is required for anything worth having in their lives.

Another author, J. K. Rowling, not that long ago made big headlines, including a cover story in *Time* magazine, with her Harry Potter books. According to the publisher Scholastic in 2019, more than 400 million copies of Harry Potter titles have been sold worldwide, and they've been translated into 68 languages. Rowling is now a multimillionaire. From most of the print media articles, it appeared that rags-to-riches Rowling, who also did a lot of her writing in coffee bars, had become a success almost overnight. Little mention was made of her effort, patience, and perseverance. In fact, her first book had taken more than five years to write.

To put things into perspective, I was a "struggling poverty case" for ten years, between 1981 and 1991, from the time I was thirty-two years old to forty-two years old. I made a total of around $85,000 during those ten years — an average income of around $8,500 per year (way below the poverty line for a single person). But let's be clear. I hardly thought of myself as poverty stricken for those ten years. To a large degree, prosperity is a state of mind.

Indeed, a lack of money can be a positive motivator and contribute to one's prosperity. As H. Jackson Brown Jr. stated in his best-selling *Life's Little Instruction Book*, "When starting out, don't worry about not having enough money. Limited funds are a blessing, not a curse. Nothing encourages creative thinking in quite the same way." In the same vein, American minister and author Norman Vincent Peale remarked, "Empty pockets never held anyone back. Only empty heads and empty hearts can do that."

Always keep in mind that having to show patience and face some difficulties on the road to success has a positive side. Arrival will feel really good. If you have never had much money in your life, attaining wealth through your own efforts will bring you a hundred times more satisfaction than being born into riches brings someone else.

FOR THE TRULY LAZY:

Be careful with your expectations.

Enormous expectations are a chief cause of discontent in this world.

The great things that you are expecting may not be expecting you.

Whenever your expectations are excessive, what you want and what you are going to get in life will end up being two vastly different things.

More Wisdom for Being a Creative Lazy Achiever:

All are inclined to believe what they covet, from a lottery-ticket up to a passport to Paradise.
— LORD BYRON

If all our happiness is bound up entirely in our personal circumstances it is difficult not to demand of life more than it has to give.
— BERTRAND RUSSELL

YOU CAN'T ALWAYS GET WHAT YOU WANT, BUT YOU CAN GET A LOT MORE THAN YOU THINK YOU CAN

As you watch the Porches, Mercedes, Lexuses, and BMWs cruise Broadway, it's easy to think that you are missing out on the good things that this world has to offer. You may yearn — as I sometimes do when I am not thinking clearly — for a brand-new red Mercedes or Porsche convertible. If you want to find out for sure whether owning a new, sleek sports car would bring you more joy in life, then you have to do what it takes to get one.

To be sure, you can't get enough money to buy everything in the world. In fact, the rest of us would be pretty hostile if you did. Like most people, however, you are probably limiting yourself in what you can accomplish and acquire in this world. Although you can't always get what you want, you can get a lot more than you think you can. An expensive sports car is something you can acquire if it's important enough to add to your feeling of success.

An important question is, Do you today think of yourself as successful or unsuccessful? Any feeling of being unsuccessful will limit the success you attain in the future. Success begets success — but not necessarily in the way most people believe. People think that to easily attain success of the highest degree, they must have already attained at least moderate success. This can result in a Catch-22. Believing that you have to be moderately successful before you attain more significant success will prevent you from achieving even moderate success.

In fact, you can obtain significant success regardless of how little success you have already. Just thinking that you are successful with what others would consider to be little success will put you in the frame of mind to attain much more success.

Your perception of being successful with whatever you presently have — money, possessions, accomplishments, and talent — will motivate you to seek other things you would like. With a positive frame of mind, you will achieve these things a lot easier.

FOR THE TRULY LAZY:

Life will always be a major disappointment when you expect to get everything you want.

Wise people tell us that learning to be content without some of the things we desire is essential for achieving success and happiness in this world.

More Wisdom for Being a Creative Lazy Achiever:

Hope is itself a species of happiness, and, perhaps, the chief happiness which this world affords: but, like all other pleasures immoderately enjoyed, the excesses of hope must be expiated by pain; and expectations improperly indulged must end in disappointment.
— *SAMUEL JOHNSON*

Nothing sets a person up more than having something turn out just the way it's supposed to be, like falling into a Swiss snowdrift and seeing a big dog come up with a little cask of brandy round its neck.
— *CLAUD COCKBURN*

A good idea is to record in a little black book all the assets and accomplishments to your credit. This can include all your educational accomplishments, your work accomplishments, and your athletic accomplishments. Don't be reserved with the truth. Include all the good things others have said about you. Consider for your success list even the number of quality friends you have made.

Whenever you are feeling down and unsuccessful, review your success list. Congratulate yourself for all your achievements, regardless of how small they may be. In no time, you will realize how successful you really are in the present — and can be in the future. Just feeling successful with what you have will put you in the inspirational frame of mind to pursue success in areas of your life that you may have been avoiding.

Another barrier to success is our unwillingness to accept that the world just may be willing to give us many of the things we want. More than being afraid of failure, we are frightened by the possibility of success. Oddly enough, some of us don't want to give up negative beliefs that have been a large part of our lives for a long time. The behaviors of criticizing successful people, complaining about our lousy circumstances, and envying talented individuals would have to be sacrificed for a more positive view of the world. We find it easier to remain in a familiar, negative comfort zone than to opt for a strange, positive one.

The world offers us a lot — not on a silver platter, but in great opportunities. Unfortunately, some of us are blind toward the opportunities that come our way. To capitalize on these opportunities and get the things we want, we must believe we deserve them; we must develop self-worth. We must realize that we have the talent and creativity to get more out of life than we are presently getting.

This is always the Creative Lazy Achiever's strategy: to find the fastest and easiest way to get where one wants to go. Operating closer to our potentials is the key to capitalizing on more of the opportunities that life throws us. People truly victimized by a poor upbringing, lousy luck, bad health, poverty, and little formal education have been incredibly successful. Yet people with many good

FOR THE TRULY LAZY:

You can't get all that you want, but do not let this keep you from getting the many things that you are capable of getting.

Whatever your aspirations and limitations, you can get a lot more than you think you can.

You will have to be highly creative — and work at least a moderate amount — to obtain them, however.

More Wisdom for Being a Creative Lazy Achiever:

God gives every bird his worm, but He does not throw it into the nest.
— P. D. JAMES

Want what you have — and you will always get what you want.
— WERNER ERHARD

breaks, right family backgrounds, proper upbringing, high formal education, plenty of financing, and great health have screwed up their lives beyond belief.

Unfortunately, psychologists state that most people aren't even close to operating at their full potential. In fact, most people don't even know their potential. And not operating close to potential is certain to hinder us from getting what we want in life.

In this regard, I know my limitations as a writer. My writing abilities will never approach those of George Bernard Shaw or that of any other Nobel Prize winner. Indeed, giving me the Nobel Prize in literature would lead to one of the biggest controversies in the world's literary community ever.

On the other hand, I won't allow my limitations to stop me from writing the books that I am capable of writing. Notwithstanding my having failed a first-year university English course three times in a row, I know that I can accomplish more as a writer than millions of people who have three times my ability. I realize that most talented people who want to write are too afraid of failure or too distracted with life's frivolities to attempt a book.

Like many people, you may have had this thought about a best-selling book on the *New York Times* list: "I could have written a book better than this one." Yes, you probably could have. So why didn't you? This also applies to any other person's accomplishment that you are capable of duplicating or surpassing. Especially if you have always wanted to achieve in that particular area, you are selling yourself short by sitting back and talking about it.

Ultimately, getting much more of what we want is not all that difficult. It's not so much a matter of being exceptional compared to others or of working long and hard hours. Instead, it's a matter of how effectively and efficiently we utilize what we have. This means putting our talents, skills, and available resources to the best possible use.

What things are you good at? What things could you be good at? Perhaps you are good with people or numbers. You may be creative, artistic, well organized, a good leader, or a great motivator. Whatever your abilities and potential abilities, you could put them to good use in earning more money and getting the things you want.

FOR THE TRULY LAZY:

Above all, there are three things that will help you get what you truly want out of life:

The first is a great attitude.

The second is the same as the first.

And the third is the same as the first two.

More Wisdom for Being a Creative Lazy Achiever:

And whatsoever ye do, do it heartily.
— THE BIBLE, COLOSSIANS 3:23

Man's rise or fall, success or failure, happiness or unhappiness, depends on his attitude . . . a man's attitude will create the situation he imagines.
— MUHAMMAD ALI

Although most people are too unmotivated to creatively put their talents, skills, and resources to better use, a lot of us are not. Being in the latter group will bring you many things you want in life, including satisfaction and happiness. Contrarily, being in the former group will give you high blood pressure, ensure that you remain in a lousy job, and keep you living in that dump in Loser Village. To be sure, emptiness and dejection often catch up with people who sit around waiting for the world to smother them with riches, meaning, success, and happiness.

By choosing to be in the former group, you make it a lot easier for those of us who are in the latter group. Less competition is something we don't mind. If you don't want to claim your share of the finer things in life, people in our group of Creative Lazy Achievers will gladly add it to our share. Abraham Lincoln had a few words to say regarding this matter: "Things may come to those who wait, but only the things left by those who hustle."

HARD WORK IS NO MATCH FOR RELAXED, CREATIVE ACTION

You have been told the hard and simple truth: if you aren't getting much out of life emotionally and financially, then you must look at what you bring into life. Clearly, to get more out of this world, you must make some important changes in your life.

Now for the pleasant truth: success has little to do with hard work. The natural order of the world doesn't dictate that you have to work hard to earn a good living and get more out of life. On the contrary, working fewer hours than most people, and at a more leisurely pace, may in fact help you to get a lot more out of life — financially and emotionally.

Most people overdramatize the value of hard work for acquiring wealth and happiness. The late Joe Karbo, author of *The Lazy Man's Way to Riches*, coined the saying, "Most people are too busy earning a living to make any money." What Karbo meant was that most people are too preoccupied with their demanding and unfulfilling jobs, as well as with frivolous after-hour

FOR THE TRULY LAZY:

Clearly, you can't run away from a bad attitude.

No matter where you go, you will encounter the same persistent troublemaker messing up your life.

Every morning, ask yourself, "How's my attitude today?"

If it isn't great, give yourself an attitude change.

More Wisdom for Being a Creative Lazy Achiever:

He was a self-made man who owed his lack of success to nobody.
— JOSEPH HELLER

If . . . you can't be a good example, then you'll just have to be a horrible warning.
— CATHERINE AIRD

activities, to devote some creative effort toward generating alternative, less demanding means of income.

In truth, the most difficult way to make a good living is to work hard for it. Hard work is no match for relaxed, creative action. Unlike people who preach the virtues of hard work, the Creative Lazy Achiever knows that important, imaginative projects lead to a lot more impressive financial results and personal satisfaction than does working long and hard. By choosing to be a Creative Lazy Achiever, you become a peak performer. You don't have to work hard to make a decent living; you have to work smart, however.

Poet W. H. Auden wisely expressed his views on work: "In order that people may be happy in their work, these three things are needed: They must be fit for it: they must not do too much of it: and they must have a sense of success in it." The second of Auden's three ingredients is the one that most people in the modern world overlook and violate. Most people in Western societies today put way too much time into their work lives and not enough into their personal lives.

With all the modern technology at our disposal, none of us need slave away to the extent that people did twenty or fifty years ago. Greater opportunity to seek a balanced and wholesome lifestyle exists now more than ever in the history of humankind; unfortunately, most people are too uncreative or too afraid of freedom to benefit, however. Today's prosperous times should be able to support millions of people seeking their true selves through creative pursuits and self-expression while working only a few hours a day.

Sadly, we would be hard-pressed to find one person in twenty who is working only four hours a day or taking a one-year sabbatical to relax and enjoy life. Paradoxically, more people actually seek their true selves in bad times than in good times. This is because many unemployed people have free time on their hands to do something other than work.

Incidentally, forced unemployment is what got me started on my quest for the truly balanced life that now allows me to work less than half the hours that most people work. I was fired from my job as an engineer after I took some vacation time without approval. Partly by choice and partly because of a

FOR THE TRULY LAZY:

Alter your thoughts and behavior and not only will you change yourself, you will change the world around you.

Whatever psychic energy you put into the universe will be reflected back to you.

The more positive energy you put into imagining and creating a happy and successful life, the more that energy will manifest itself in the real world.

More Wisdom for Being a Creative Lazy Achiever:

There are in life as many aspects as attitudes towards it, and aspects change with attitudes.
— *KATHERINE MANSFIELD*

The greatest discovery of my generation is that man can alter his life simply by altering his attitude of mind.
— *WILLIAM JAMES*

recession, I wound up being unemployed for two years. My firing turned out to be the best thing that ever happened in my engineering career. I subsequently went through a transformation that put me on course for the relaxed lifestyle that I enjoy today.

Contrary to popular belief, not everyone today works hard to earn a comfortable living. In percentages, the number of these non-hard-workers is relatively small; in actual numbers, the figure is quite large. Although I estimate this group to be about 5 percent of the working population in Western countries, let's say that it's only 2 percent. Given that the working population of the United States is about two hundred million, about four million Americans would be working at a more relaxed pace. The numbers are probably higher. These unusual workers are spread throughout the United States (as in all Western nations), hidden among the hard-core Workaholics and the Nine-to-Fivers not ambitious enough to search for something better.

Although most people in practically all occupational fields work hard and long hours, some individuals in each of these occupations work just a few hours a day. Take, for example, the late writer W. Somerset Maugham.

Most authors work long and hard hours. Maugham sat down to write every morning at 9:30 A.M. and quit at 1:00 P.M., however. Then he had a martini before lunch. After lunch, he did absolutely nothing in the way of work.

You may ask, "Didn't it hurt Maugham to work only three-and-a-half hours a day?" Not at all! Toward the end of his career, he lived in a villa in Cap Ferrat with an outdoor pool. He employed a staff of fourteen, including a butler, a chauffeur, two maids, and seven gardeners. Not bad for a slacker!

In the same vein, although consultants, lawyers, engineers, doctors, and dentists are known for their long hours at work, not all people in these professions follow the status quo. A small percentage work thirty to thirty-five hours a week and make a decent living. They accomplish this by running their own practices and working smart instead of hard.

By keeping overhead low, minimizing paperwork, and using time and materials efficiently, these professionals are able to make up to 80 percent of the incomes that other professionals in their industry make working two or

FOR THE TRULY LAZY:

Anyone can achieve something important.

Contrary to popular belief, the key is not working hard — but finding the right thing to achieve.

More Wisdom for Being a Creative Lazy Achiever:

We live at a time when man believes himself fabulously capable of creation, but he does not know what to create.
— *JOSE ORTEGAY GASSET*

The really efficient laborer will be found not to crowd his day with work, but will saunter to his task surrounded by a wide halo of ease and leisure.
— *HENRY DAVID THOREAU*

No great man ever complains of want of opportunities.
— *RALPH WALDO EMERSON*

three times the number of hours. Moreover, because these relaxed professionals have put money and possessions in their proper place, they control their personal spending better than do their hardworking colleagues. They thus actually acquire more wealth even if their incomes are lower.

With more than four million people in the United States working smart instead of hard, surely more people can do the same. This includes you, whether you live in the United States or in any other Western nation. Just because most people are flattening their noses against the grindstone, you don't have to flatten yours as well. I don't know about you, but I would look funny — even ridiculous — with a flat nose. That's why I am no longer in good standing with the hard workers of this world.

You probably know someone like me who has less talent or education than you do but who doesn't seem to need to work so hard to make a living. This in itself should be sufficient to convince you that you are capable of the same.

Perhaps the skeptic in you will ask, "If it can be done by more people, why aren't they doing it?" In fact, a lot more people can do it. The reason they aren't is that they aren't prepared to make the sacrifices and put in the creative effort to get there. People will tolerate unreasonable demands from employers to work unpaid overtime in boring, low-paying, dead-end jobs simply because staying put is easier than walking away. Moreover, there is much greater security in doing the familiar than in doing something different.

The same skeptic in you may now go one step further and ask, "What would happen to the world if everyone worked only four or five hours a day?" The answer is, "The world would definitely be a better place to live — less stress, less frustration, more healthy people, more happy people, and less environmental damage." You don't have to worry about everyone else doing that, however. To be sure, most North Americans aren't prepared to pay the price to find out how to do it.

The good news is that you can take advantage of the fact that 95 percent of all individuals are too unmotivated to get to the state where they are working smart instead of hard. This makes it easier for you to be one of the 2 to 5 percent of workers who lead a relaxed and balanced lifestyle and still end up

FOR THE TRULY LAZY:

It has yet to be proven that hard work guarantees success.

Millions of people have started at the bottom, worked hard for years, and stayed at the bottom.

To avoid ending up like them, base your actions on critical thinking, creative thinking, and common sense instead of hard work.

Doing so will make you infinitely more likely to succeed in life.

More Wisdom for Being a Creative Lazy Achiever:

We live in the age of the overworked, and the under-educated; the age in which people are so industrious that they become absolutely stupid.
— OSCAR WILDE

Success is simple. Do what's right, the right way, at the right time.
— ARNOLD GLASOW

feeling prosperous. To accomplish this, you must remove whatever limitations you have imposed upon yourself as an individual. Only then will you be able to spot the opportunities that exist for you to work only four or five hours a day.

Having lived a relaxed lifestyle for more than twenty years, I must warn you about the occupational hazards of working smart and not hard. These include having to deal with freedom, responsibility, and joy in life. You must also deal with envy from the pathological critics and complainers of the world. When you reach a time when you are working only four hours a day, you will be looked upon as a threat to capitalism and the stability of the modern world. If you can handle these occupational hazards, drop by one of my favorite coffee bars. We can have an interesting conversation — while the uncreative working stiffs keep their noses to the grindstone in the hope of attaining freedom, joy, and satisfaction thirty or forty years in the future.

3C VISION WILL HELP MAKE YOU MORE SUCCESSFUL THAN 3D VISION

It's worth repeating. To be more successful, try working less and thinking more. That's what I do. As a self-published author whose books have sold over 1,000,000 copies and have earned around $3 million in pretax profits, I am more successful and prosperous than 99.5 percent of authors. I have attained financial independence and personal freedom that the vast majority of authors would like to attain. To be clear about this, it has nothing to do with luck.

On October 15, 2019 *Publishers Weekly* reported that the total number of print and ebooks that were self-published in 2018 was 1.68 million, up from 1.19 million in 2017. Apparently any wannabe best-selling author can now afford to preach in the desert. What do you think the average sales for those self-published books will be? Just recently, book marketing expert Brian Jud stated, "According to BookScan, 93 percent of all new books do not sell more than 100 copies." My seventeen books have sold an average of 61,176 copies.

What's the secret to my success? It's certainly not "hard work." For the record, I believe in outsmarting my competition instead of outworking my

FOR THE TRULY LAZY:

Everyone at birth was given his or her own Personal Common Sense User's Kit.

Many individuals don't remember where they put it.

Others haven't figured out what to do with it.

More Wisdom for Being a Creative Lazy Achiever:

Most people are such fools that it is really no great compliment to say that someone is above the average.
— *W. SOMERSET MAUGHAM*

The first principle is that you must not fool yourself — and you are the easiest person to fool.
— *RICHARD FEYNMAN*

Darwin will sort out the delusional, pig-headed, and willfully ignorant.
— *MARK COKER*

competition. Outsmarting my competition requires 3C Vision and not 3D Vision. Problem is, in today's Internet dumbed-down, feel-good 21st century Western world, many people are operating with 3D Vision. Their 3D Vision — deflative, dreadful, and destructive — is based on these three elements:

1. Delusion
2. Denial
3. Distortion

On the other hand, my 3C Vision — contemplative, cheerful, and constructive — is based on these three elements:

1. Critical thinking skills
2. Creative thinking skills
3. Common sense

Just a warning that we all have to be a little careful in assessing whether we as individuals possess the three elements of 3C Vision. Cornell University psychology professors, Justin Kruger and David Dunning, have done extensive research on the topic of incompetence masked by overconfidence. The result of their work has become known as the Dunning-Kruger phenomenon. In short, Dunning and Kruger contend that incompetent people often suffer from delusions of superiority that result in their vastly overrating their own abilities. In other words, these incompetent people with no results have super 3D Vision.

Interestingly, the reason that these people have such a low level of competence is that they lack the awareness to accurately assess their own skills. Furthermore, they tend not to recognize the higher skill level in others. Many years before the research of Dunning and Kruger, British philosopher, social critic, and writer Bertrand Russell had been aware of this phenomenon when he declared, "The trouble with the world is that the stupid are cocksure and the intelligent full of doubt."

How will you know when you are operating with 3C Vision and not with 3D Vision? Easy. You will get positive, meaningful results from your thoughtful actions. Even though you will work less than the vast majority of people, you will attain a lot more success and prosperity in your life than they do in their lives. Results won't lie, in other words.

FOR THE TRULY LAZY:

To know, yet to think that you do not know, is putting yourself at a disadvantage.

Not to know, yet to think that you know, is setting yourself up for disaster.

More Wisdom for Being a Creative Lazy Achiever:

Do not delude yourself. Self-delusion is one of the greatest inventions of the human mind. It helps many people think that they are Masters of the game of life when, in fact, they are merely impostors.
— LIFE'S SECRET HANDBOOK

The less people know, the more stubbornly they know it.
— RAJNEESH (OSHO)

If I wanted to become a tramp, I would seek information and advice from the most successful tramp I could find. If I wanted to become a failure, I would seek advice from men who have never succeeded. If I wanted to succeed in all things, I would look around me for those who are succeeding, and do as they have done.
— JOSEPH MARSHALL WADE

Chapter 2

Work at

WHAT YOU ARE

and Not at

WHAT YOU AIN'T

FOR THE TRULY LAZY:

Never mistake hard work for success about to happen.

Much hard work is wasted on things that don't make any positive difference in this world.

Trying to achieve success solely through hard work is like trying to reach the North Pole by heading south.

You may eventually get there, but it will take a hundred times the energy, time, and sacrifice that it should take.

More Wisdom for Being a Creative Lazy Achiever:

The society based on production is only productive, not creative.
— *ALBERT CAMUS*

Look at me: I worked my way up from nothing to a state of extreme poverty.
— *GROUCHO MARX*

NEITHER WEALTH NOR SPLENDOR, BUT TRANQUILITY AND OCCUPATION GIVE HAPPINESS

Your overall success in life depends on many things. To a significant degree, it depends upon how well you earn your living. How well you earn your living is determined by how much you enjoy your work. This shouldn't be a shocking revelation to most people. Surprisingly, however, even after all that has been written in the last few years about the importance of choosing enjoyable and satisfying work, many people ignore this wisdom.

Some people even preach the opposite. In his best-selling book *Die Broke*, financial adviser Stephen M. Pollan advocates that you forget about career satisfaction and "view your job primarily as an income-generating device." Although Pollan has written an excellent book overall, most career advisers strongly disagree with the author's contention that you should continually move to the highest-paid job available and forget about trying to find self-fulfillment at work.

If you follow Pollan's strategy, you will set yourself up for career failure. If you aren't working at something you enjoy, you are settling for much less than you deserve. It is no secret that the happiest and most successful people at work have great affection for their selected vocation. Generally speaking, they are also the most successful in the long term.

Sacrificing present-day well-being for too long can only lead to dire consequences down the road. Most obvious of these, your long-term well-being will never materialize. Continually sacrificing your present-day satisfaction and happiness generally ensures that you never will experience present-day satisfaction and happiness. In the worst-case scenario, the undertaker will attend to you many years earlier than he should.

There must be more to work — and life in general — than just earning a good living. You can only feel prosperous insofar as you experience happiness today and do not sacrifice everything for a joyful tomorrow that will probably

FOR THE TRULY LAZY:

Trust not what inspires other members of society to choose a career.

Trust what inspires you.

From this decision alone will come over a third of your satisfaction or misery in your life.

More Wisdom for Being a Creative Lazy Achiever:

The best augury of a man's success in his profession is that he thinks it the finest in the world.
— GEORGE ELIOT

Success is not the key to happiness. Happiness is the key to success. If you love what you are doing, you will be successful.
— ALBERT SCHWEITZERT

I believe you are your work. Don't trade the stuff of your life, time, for nothing more than dollars. That's a rotten bargain.
— RITA MAE BROWN

never arrive. Because you need to spend so much of your life working, it's important to make your career satisfying and fulfilling.

Even if your goal is to work only four or five hours a day, high priorities should include job satisfaction, a healthy work environment, and some sense of control in your job. In case you haven't noticed, there will be plenty of life's unexpected events to test you without your having to work in a lousy job.

Far too many people today work long hours at jobs they terribly dislike. These people are motivated to get up in the morning by a paycheck and by little else. An accountant who makes $60,000 a year in a dead-end job is experiencing a fulfillment deficit; so is a university professor who makes $150,000 a year but who dislikes lecturing to students. Both cases represent career failure of the highest order.

Many of today's jobs even have fancy titles to go along with the good pay. Nothing in these positions supports satisfaction and creative achievement, however. Paper pushing is paper pushing, regardless of the job title that goes along with it. This applies not only to clerical jobs; many well-paid management positions, complete with the most modern laptop computers, are simply glorified paper-pushing jobs. A fancy job title tricks employees into feeling better about their positions, but as former U.S. senator George McGovern has stated, "The longer the job title, the less important the job."

Unfortunately, most individuals choose their jobs and careers based on what society, educational institutions, and their parents advise them to pursue. These decisions are influenced by the power, status, prestige, and level of pay the jobs offer, instead of by the enjoyment and satisfaction they could provide. Consequently, North America is full of stupendously intelligent, well-educated, highly trained, and extraordinarily skilled people who have yet to experience any measurable career success in their lives. Career success, for the purposes of this book, is having gratifying work that is both personally and financially rewarding.

To the surprise of many, the majority of people even in the most prestigious of professions experience career dissatisfaction. Despite the status and high income of the legal profession, for example, few lawyers find fulfillment and

FOR THE TRULY LAZY:

The best advice that anyone can give you for choosing a specific career is never to accept someone else's advice.

Indeed, one of the biggest reasons for choosing the career you have chosen should be that no one told you to.

More Wisdom for Being a Creative Lazy Achiever:

We only do well the things we like doing.
— COLETTE

Most people perform essentially meaningless work. When they retire that truth is borne upon them.
— BRENDAN FRANCIS

Give to the world the best you have and the best will come back to you.
— MADELINE BRIDGES

satisfaction in their jobs. An ex-lawyer friend stated that one of his classmates and he couldn't name one person from their law class who truly enjoyed being a lawyer.

John Grisham, ex-lawyer turned best-selling author, echoed this comment. Grisham told a reporter that he doesn't know of one lawyer who does not want to get into something better. We can only hope that we will see the day when lawyers have outplayed their usefulness to the rest of society so that fewer people are dissatisfied with their jobs and, of course, so that we don't have to deal with them again.

Like most lawyers, many people get into high-paying jobs, at the expense of job satisfaction, to feel prosperous and build wealth for the future. Ironically, dissatisfaction with a high-paying job can hinder both prosperity consciousness and wealth creation. To be sure, people can't experience much happiness in the present if they don't get satisfaction and self-fulfillment from their work. As you can imagine, it's impossible to feel prosperous when you are unhappy.

Frequently, in an attempt to feel happier and more prosperous, people in unfulfilling careers end up spending more money and saving less. Many acquire possessions as a form of therapy to deal with stress and dissatisfaction. A $35,000 sports utility vehicle may be purchased impulsively as a reward for having to cope with a crazed boss and a boring job.

Purchasing expensive therapeutic gifts may lift people's spirits temporarily, but the behavior is self-defeating, locking them into their lousy jobs. Leaving the high-paying job for a more satisfying job becomes more difficult when payments have to be made on the vehicle for another six years. Moreover, people who continually spend money on expensive therapeutic rewards for the constant job dissatisfaction they endure build little wealth.

With time, money becomes increasingly more important to the dissatisfied workers of the world. An unhealthy and aberrant obsession, money rules their lives. With no enjoyment and satisfaction at work, these people continually look to money and material possessions, not only as an escape, but as an attempt to put meaning into their lives. They cannot break the vicious work-and-spend cycle, along with an obsession with money, until they move to an

FOR THE TRULY LAZY:

Working strictly for money is not the way to true career success.

Stop and ponder money in new ways, and you will realize that many aspects of it are totally absurd.

You will also realize that, after the provision of basic necessities, happiness cares little about money.

So why do you care so much about it?

More Wisdom for Being a Creative Lazy Achiever:

We work to become, not to acquire.
— ELBERT HUBBARD

The miracle is not that we do this work, but that we are happy to do it.
— MOTHER TERESA

occupation that is fun and fulfilling. Only then can they relegate money to much lesser importance and can life become a joy instead of a struggle.

With all the emphasis our society places on money, it's easy for any one of us to get permanently imprisoned in this job-dissatisfaction trap that catches so many well-educated and intelligent people. In the pursuit of money, we overlook the fact that career success can't be guaranteed through having superior intelligence, a high level of formal education, special skills, and hard work; knowing the right people; or being in a high-status field such as law, medicine, or architecture.

In truth, we can attain career success only when we work at something that we truly enjoy and that benefits others. In no other way can we experience true satisfaction and happiness, not only in our jobs, but in our lives.

Make no mistake about it: happiness will continually elude you if you work just for money. "It is neither wealth nor splendor," advised Thomas Jefferson, "but tranquility and occupation, which give happiness." To the extent you fail to see the importance of a fulfilling career, you're unlikely to experience real meaning and have a significant purpose to your life.

If you sacrifice your present-day happiness far a meaningless job, you probably won't ever get the opportunity to experience true happiness and satisfaction from your work in the future. The longer some people are unhappy in a lousy career, the more comfortable they become being unhappy. After a while, they forget what it is like to be happy; they actually think it is normal to be unhappy. You must avoid this situation; otherwise, like many lawyers, you will remain unhappy and dissatisfied for the rest of your life.

Only you can answer if your present career is an asset or a liability. To be sure, working in a high-paying job that you enjoy immensely is ideal. Using the standards of the Creative Lazy Achiever, this puts your career overwhelmingly on the asset side. Your career is on the verge of being a liability when you are underpaid for something you enjoy doing. It is definitely a liability in terms of your prosperity-consciousness and overall life energy when you dislike what you are doing. This is true regardless of how much money you are paid.

FOR THE TRULY LAZY:

The problem with secure jobs is that once you have read the morning paper, you have nothing creative, constructive, or stimulating left to do.

You will never experience satisfaction at work until you direct your physical and mental energy toward something that makes a big difference.

This means that you must have a purpose much higher than working for the biggest paycheck possible.

More Wisdom for Being a Creative Lazy Achiever:

Only passions, great passions, can elevate the soul to great things.
— DENIS DIDEROT

He did it with all his heart, and prospered.
— THE BIBLE, II CHRONICLES 31:21

Another test of whether your job costs too much in terms of dissatisfaction and unhappiness is whether you would be willing to do it for another few years if you were to become financially independent today. If your impulse would be to quit immediately, you are undoubtedly in the wrong job. Here is still another test for the true value of your present job: if your two favorite times at work are lunchtime and quitting time, it's time to move on.

No doubt you will want to rationalize that staying put is better for your well-being than trying something more interesting and challenging. Sure, keeping that well-paid job ensures that you can pay the mortgage, keep the second car, get the family expensive Christmas presents, purchase that bigscreen TV, and send the kids to summer camp. You must decide, however, whether you truly need all those extras in life for which you are sacrificing your creative expression and the opportunity to make a difference in the world.

Clearly, you won't have a complete life until you have work that really matters to you. Leaving a well-established job for a new, interesting, and challenging occupation may be difficult, but it is not impossible. Millions have done it, and so can you.

After reading *The Joy of Not Working*, several people, most married and with children, either sent letters or called to tell me that they had quit their secure jobs to pursue what they were meant to do. The book was the catalyst they needed to pursue something much more interesting and fulfilling. Some of these people have contacted me a second and third time to let me know that they are happier and doing just fine financially. They claim that the freedom and opportunity to be spontaneous and creative has made it all worthwhile.

Nothing can keep you imprisoned in a job as much as the fear that you won't be able to make as much money somewhere else. To combat the dangers of career rigor mortis brought on by security-consciousness, you must attenuate your immediate need for money. The less interested you are in the pursuit of money and material possessions, the more latitude and choice you will have for a fulfilling career.

Once you break free from seeing money as an end in itself, a whole new world opens up. The paradox is that when you utilize your talents to pursue

FOR THE TRULY LAZY:

Working efficiently is key, but you must be working at what is right for you.

Clearly, you won't excel in any field unless you enjoy what you are doing immensely.

Do whatever you must to work at what's right for you, because a day of work you hate will seem like an eternity compared to a month of work you love.

More Wisdom for Being a Creative Lazy Achiever:

Happy are those who dream dreams and are ready to pay the price to make them come true.
— *LEON J. SUENES*

You are what you do. If you do boring, stupid, monotonous work, chances are you'll end up boring, stupid, and monotonous.
— *BOB BLACK*

something you enjoy, without regard to making a lot of money, several byproducts result; one common by-product is that you make a lot of money. Statistics indicate that people who enjoy their work end up making more money in the long term than people who go into a career just to make money.

Mark Albion, in his book *Making a Life, Making a Living; Reclaiming Your Purpose and Passion in Business and Life*, cites a study that followed the careers of 1,500 business-school graduates. Upon graduation in 1960, 1,245 of the graduates said that their first priority was to make good money so that they could do what they wanted to do later in life. The other 255 decided to pursue what they liked with hopes that the money would follow. Of 101 of the people who became millionaires by 1980, only one belonged to the former group.

To the degree that you have an enjoyable career and are committed to pursuing it with passion and excellence, earning a good living is not all that difficult. Consider what it would be like to do half as much work for twice or three times the money. This is what is possible in the long term when you work at what you enjoy.

You will no doubt do your best work when you are motivated by some important purpose other than money. Making money becomes a great deal more difficult when you make it your major purpose. Indeed, people seldom succeed at anything worthwhile unless they enjoy it. Not only that, but those people working at something they don't enjoy display a lack of self-confidence. They have the false belief that they don't have the talent, creativity, or courage to earn money at something they enjoy.

In summary, a full, relaxed, satisfying, and happy life can be enjoyed only in the present and is attainable only when you enjoy what you do for a living. You experience success in your career when you work for the love of it, for personal fulfillment, or as a commitment to making the world a better place. Meaning and a rewarding experience of work are readily available provided money and status are not your top priorities. Ultimately, challenging, gratifying work will be both personally and financially rewarding, because money comes much faster when you pursue what you value and truly enjoy.

FOR THE TRULY LAZY:

Everything keeps its best character by being put to its best use.

This applies to both people and things.

Thus, choose work in harmony with your character and values.

For anything short of this, you are cheating yourself out of eight hours of happiness and satisfaction each workday.

More Wisdom for Being a Creative Lazy Achiever:

If you follow the crowd, you will likely get no further than the crowd. If you walk alone, you're likely to end up in places no one has ever been before. Being an achiever is not without its difficulties, for peculiarity breeds contempt. The unfortunate thing about being ahead of your time is that when people finally realize you were right, they'll simply say it was obvious to everyone all along. You have two choices in life. You can dissolve into the main stream, or you can choose to become an achiever and be distinct. To be distinct, you must be different. To be different, you must strive to be what no else but you can be.

— ALAN ASHLEY-PITT

IT'S NOT WHAT YOU BECOME, BUT WHAT YOU DON'T BECOME THAT WILL HURT MOST IN THE END

Given the choice between pursuing a cherished dream or continuing a life of grindstone existence, most people opt for the grindstone existence. They tolerate abusive bosses, lousy working conditions, and boring, dead-end jobs simply because finding a better job takes time and energy. Moreover, pursuing a career dream requires changing and taking risks. Most people find it easier to stay with the familiar, even if the familiar offers nothing more than boredom and drudgery.

Sadly, many people on their deathbeds reflect upon their lives with deep sorrow. Not having followed their career dreams is usually their biggest regret. Besides missing out on enjoyment and prosperity-consciousness now, if you aren't pursuing your career dreams today, you are setting yourself up for the same disappointment and regrets later in life.

You probably have dreams that you want to pursue and skills and talents that you would like to utilize somewhere in your work. You may have suppressed these skills and talents for some time because you have been obsessed with making as much money as possible, in the shortest period of time. It's important to contemplate the wisdom of this Chinese adage as it relates to your dreams: "If you get on the train today, you'll overpay your fare. But if you don't, you'll be left behind in the dust."

Perhaps you realize that you can lead a more meaningful, more fulfilling, and happier existence only if you make important changes in your life. All along, however, you have put off making a change because you are waiting for the perfect moment, with the right conditions. Clearly, there will never be the perfect moment.

Waiting for things to get better will ensure that they don't get better. To wish your life away in anticipation of living some long-awaited dream sometime in the distant future is to do yourself a great disservice. That future

FOR THE TRULY LAZY:

The way to shun success is to specialize in the areas of your greatest weakness and dislike.

You are more likely to be a winner when you are selective about the races you enter.

Ensure that you place your efforts where they matter most.

Stick to the tasks that you are good at and that you truly enjoy.

More Wisdom for Being a Creative Lazy Achiever:

Nothing great was ever achieved without enthusiasm.
— RALPH WALDO EMERSON

Life without absorbing occupation is hell.
— ELBERT HUBBARD

may never come — and in the event that it doesn't, you will never get satisfaction from the things that you intended to accomplish. Clearly, whether your vocational dreams include fame, creative accomplishment, or adventure, today is the time to start working toward those dreams.

You may have worked yourself up the ladder from nurse to head administrator of New York's biggest hospital, for example, only to realize that you would rather live in a loft in SoHo and make a living as an artist. Alternatively, you may be working sixteen hours a day repairing safety helmets for an environmental corporation in northern Canada when deep down you want to be like your writer friends who are part of the Starbuck's laptop-and-cappuccino crowd. Whatever you think intuitively that you should be doing, you should give it some serious consideration and explore the possibilities.

The goal is to have your work be the principal expression for your mind and creative talent. You can put your purpose, talents, character, and dreams into a career in many ways if you use your imagination. Many options and opportunities await you, provided you look for them. Only you can determine what you want specifically, however, and only you can put yourself in the right direction toward getting it. In the words of Walt Whitman, "Not I — not anyone else — can travel that road for you. You must travel it for yourself."

When choosing a new career, you must make every effort possible to select one that is right for you. "Do not put your spoon into the pot that doesn't boil for you," advises a Romanian proverb. Your pot will boil for you when your career allows you to pursue some important purpose that can make a difference in this world. A proper career should also allow you to utilize the special talents that you want to use. To really work for you, your career should be compatible with your character and the lifestyle you would like to lead.

Like most people, you may think that your dream of working in an interesting and exciting occupation is frivolous and beyond the realm of your skill and talent. In this case, you are doing yourself a great disservice by placing limitations on what you can accomplish in this world. It is in your long-term best interest to consider the words of Henry David Thoreau: "I have learned this at least by my experiment: that if one advances confidently in the

FOR THE TRULY LAZY:

Find out what you are most suited for and focus on it.

Put your energy where the satisfaction is, not where it isn't.

Achieving mediocre results on the right, interesting projects will bring you a lot more happiness than achieving outstanding results on the wrong, uninteresting ones.

More Wisdom for Being a Creative Lazy Achiever:

I'd rather be a failure at something I enjoy than a success at something I hate.
— GEORGE BURNS

Success means only doing what you do well, letting someone else do the rest.
— GOLDSTEIN S. TRUISM

direction of his dreams, and endeavors to live the life which he has imagined, he will meet with a success unexpected in common hours."

Career dreams do come true for people, but only for self-confident individuals who constantly focus and work on them. Look around, and you will see many individuals living their vocational dreams. People have turned their hobbies into part-time businesses that have eventually become multimillion dollar businesses. Others have given up careers for which they have been highly educated to pursue careers for which they have had no education. Even with this disadvantage, they have been able to turn their dreams into realities and create abundance in their lives.

For some of us already working toward our dreams, direction becomes an issue. This is best depicted by the Jewish people's folktale about a man searching for a place called Paradise. Every night before going to bed, this man points his boots toward his goal. Each morning, he steps into his boots and continues merrily along his journey toward Paradise. Unfortunately, a year later, during the night, a mischievous imp turns his boots around. The next day, the man thinks he's headed for Paradise, but he's really headed in the opposite direction. In another year, he ends up back where he started.

It's easy to become this misguided man. We can be highly motivated and put in a lot of effort in an attempt to reach some wonderful goal or dream. In a rapidly changing world, our environment and circumstances change quickly, and distractions are tempting.

Somewhere along the way, when we aren't paying attention, we may easily become sidetracked without realizing it. The fact that we are continuing from where we left off yesterday doesn't mean that we are headed in the right direction today. Even if our goals and dreams haven't changed, it's prudent to evaluate our present position regularly to ensure that we are still headed in the right direction.

One of the greatest distractions in our lives must be the financial traps into which we so easily fall. Obsession with money and material gain distracts us from our purpose, goals, and dreams. In the same vein, the need for immediate gratification through the latest material possessions puts us at odds with our

FOR THE TRULY LAZY:

Work at what you are and not at what you ain't.

Nothing is more a waste of time than trying to be what you are not and can never happily be.

Do what you are most suited for, and you will succeed with the least amount of stress and effort.

This is the Creative Lazy Achiever's way: attain success in the healthiest and most relaxed way possible.

More Wisdom for Being a Creative Lazy Achiever:

Be certain of this law of the Universe: Success will elude you as long as you are doing what's wrong for you; and needless to say, success will come easily when you are doing what's right for you.

— LIFE'S SECRET HANDBOOK

real purpose of doing something satisfying and making a difference in the world. To ensure that we are not left behind in our quest for the latest material comforts, we buy the biggest and the best things, even though we can't afford them. In this way, we perpetuate the financial binds that compromise our ability to fully pursue our dreams.

Even when you are quite sure that you are pursuing what you were meant to pursue, it is worthwhile to step back regularly to evaluate your progress. Because we continually change as human beings, our priorities sometimes change without us being fully conscious of it. Evaluation should be a constant process to ensure that our important needs are being met and that we are satisfied with our job.

Long ago, you may have decided that your heart's desire was to be a criminal lawyer, for example, yet now you may realize that you really want to write science fiction novels. Or perhaps your purpose at one time was to make as much money as possible, but now you realize that you need something with a little more meaning. The ideal is always to work at something that makes a difference, to do the things you enjoy, and to use your most cherished talents,

Whatever you would like to do, you must set in motion the forces that will get you there. The longer you put off pursuing your dream of a fulfilling career, the more time becomes your enemy. Time will steal your vocational dreams if you keep waiting for the right moment. Keep in mind that you can get more money, but you can't get more time.

Years from now, as you reflect upon your life, you don't want to regret not having earned your living by singing, designing software, working with children, building things with your hands, traveling to new cities, or inspiring others to new heights. It may hurt a little to discover that you have only dreamed about the interesting life filled with spontaneity and creativity. It may hurt a lot, in fact. An unknown wise person once advised that the ache of unfulfilled dreams can be the worst pain you ever experience.

FOR THE TRULY LAZY:

Do not specialize in the insignificant if you want to be a master of the significant.

This is the most important principle for people who achieve greatness in their careers.

It is extremely important — but so simple that most people overlook it.

More Wisdom for Being a Creative Lazy Achiever:

One principal reason why people are so often useless is that they neglect their own profession or calling, and divide and shift their attention among a multitude of objects and pursuits.
— *NATHANIEL EMMONS*

Forget about destiny. You don't need destiny to soar to greater heights. You need to tune into higher frequencies.
— *LIFE'S SECRET HANDBOOK*

CONTROLLING YOUR DESTINY IS MORE IMPORTANT THAN THE SIZE OF YOUR PAYCHECK

Prosperity-consciousness and the experience of being a peak performer will come to you when you are in control of your life. Given that you do have to work for a living, you still must have as much control as possible over your job — which, of course, gives you more control over your life. Especially if you value your creativity, freedom, and independence, control over your destiny is more important than the size of your paycheck.

Your career is a major liability in the event you have little control over your position and feel at the mercy of your work environment. You can't feel free when you are enslaved by your job and your emotions, constantly in frustration as you work to make someone else rich. Moreover, you may prefer not to experience some of the long-term implications, such as insanity, premature death, or craving the comfort of a grave like Dilbert in Scott Adam's cartoon.

Study after study indicates that people who have little control in their jobs suffer the most stress and health problems. In one of the best-known recent studies in this area, the Whitehall study conducted on British civil servants, death rates before retirement for manual workers and clerks were found to be much higher than for professionals and executives. Researchers concluded that workers with the least control over their jobs had the highest death rates; top-level administrators had the lowest.

The easiest way to succeed, then, is to maximize control over your life. Lack of control means uncertainty and stress. When you work for someone else, especially a large organization, you lose freedom, which can lead to feelings of helplessness and alienation. Interestingly, a recent study found that over 40 percent of corporate employees feel very lonely at work. Because most corporations today value short-term profits and share prices much more than they value the freedom and well-being of their workers, you will best be able to control your destiny if you break away from conventional employment.

FOR THE TRULY LAZY:

You will know when you have the right job or career.

Overall, it won't seem like work to you.

It, instead, will be enjoyment for which you get well paid.

You would gladly do the work for free — even pay handsomely to do it — if you didn't have to earn a living.

More Wisdom for Being a Creative Lazy Achiever:

It is not real work unless you would rather be doing something else.
— J. M. BARRIE

I was proud to work with the great Gershwin, and I would have done it for nothing, which I did.
— HOWARD DIETZ

This is not to say that you cannot have an interesting and enjoyable job, along with some control, working for someone else. Indeed, many people do. Most interesting corporate jobs, however, require you to work a lot more hours than you would like.

You can remain in a corporation and become "Dilbertized" along with the others. Some people don't mind being involved in circular discussions, writing unread reports, performing uncreative activities, and being ruled by the clock. As long as they have a "secure" job, they can cope for another twenty years until they achieve Pension Heaven. To others, however, working such a job does not bring security, and it certainly doesn't offer freedom. Indeed, working in such a job is more like being in prison.

Generally speaking, the best way to control your destiny is through self-employment. Researchers have confirmed that most self-employed people feel happier than people employed by others, because self-employed people control their own work hours and schedules and the types of activities in which they indulge. People who work for themselves in their own business or as a contract employee can feel a lot freer and more satisfied making $45,000 a year than a frustrated middle manager might feel making $125,000 with a Fortune 500 company. One of the biggest advantages to such self-employment is that no one tells you what to do. You have control over your workplace and flexibility in when and how you work. You can do your own thing, in your own time, in your own way.

Here's a warning, however: self-employment or business ownership is not for everyone. It takes a strong heart to break away from conventional employment. It takes faith, hope, and energy to develop a product or service and take it to market. Some people need corporations more than corporations need them. If you aren't prepared to take risks and make decisions on your own, stick to working for someone else. In this case, however, make every possible attempt to find a position that offers some latitude for controlling your job and experiencing freedom in what you do.

Having said this, I don't want to discourage you from working for yourself. Don't allow me or anyone else to talk you out of pursuing what you know to

FOR THE TRULY LAZY:

Clearly, you will always have to pay some dues before you attain anything worthwhile.

Don't believe that you have to pay the same dues in time and energy that most people pay, however.

Do not underestimate the essence, the power, and the value of your creativity.

You can climb the ladder of success rung by rung, or you can be creative and skip several rungs along the way.

More Wisdom for Being a Creative Lazy Achiever:

Listen to your answers — even when others think that these are answers of a fool. As long as your answers are your highest truths and coincide with your most cherished dreams, your answers along with creative action will lead you to your destiny where you get to express life in the divine way that the Universe meant you to.

— LIFE'S SECRET HANDBOOK

be a great idea. Providing a service or product that you truly believe in is key to making it on your own. People who experience the most freedom, prosperity, and financial independence use their creativity to develop ideas, products, and services of value to other people. And the best climate in which to do this is outside the typical workplace.

Here's another warning: don't expect your friends and family to support you when you decide to work for yourself. You will find others to be full of fear and doubt. Some people may even think you have lost your sanity when, in fact, they show signs of having lost theirs.

Studies indicate that individuals who are eventually highly successful are able to brush off rejection and unfounded criticism. These individuals are not afraid to walk away from a sure job and take a risk on a venture that promises to be a lot more exciting, interesting, and fulfilling. They may end up working just as hard for a year or two, but at least they are working for themselves. In doing so, they feel healthier, freer, and more prosperous.

As a writer and a part-time professional speaker, I can vouch for the advantages of not working for someone else. Over thirty years ago I told everyone who would listen — including an order taker at McDonald's, two derelicts on a Vancouver park bench, and a Nigerian scam artist trying to steal $2,500 from me — about my great idea for a book on how to handle leisure time. The book's title eventually became *The Joy of Not Working*. I figured that this book would launch a career for me as a successful author. Many people laughed at the idea; others seriously thought that I was crazy. As it turned out, this book was the one that put me on track to prosperity and personal freedom.

Having paid the price of searching and discovering what I want to be when I grow up, I am now doing what I enjoy most on my own terms. There is no life like it — what a great way to make a living! Why work for any one of millions of bosses when I can work for my favorite boss — me? Being on my own affords me the freedom to sleep in until noon, go visit a charming member of the opposite sex at the coffee bar, ride ten miles on my bicycle, and talk to a friend for two hours all before I start work — without being confronted by a demanding boss.

FOR THE TRULY LAZY:

No one will ever expect you to achieve the impossible.

You must not hope to be more than you can be.

It is not always possible to achieve as you want, but only as you can.

Only in knowing your limitations, and doing your best, will you come closest to perfection.

More Wisdom for Being a Creative Lazy Achiever:

There is no more futile punishment than futile and hopeless labor.
— *ALBERT CAMUS*

Never desert your own line of talent. Be what nature intended you for, and you will succeed.
— *SYDNEY SMITH*

Provided you are prepared to pay your dues, you will find many opportunities to be part of the independent laptop-and-cappuccino crowd. Some opportunities that friends and acquaintances have exploited are import/export businessperson, real-estate salesperson, management consultant, computer software designer, sessional college instructor, writer, artist, professional speaker, newsletter publisher, and freelance theater manager. Working in these fields has given many of these individuals the freedom to work smart and not hard. By practicing the principles of the Creative Lazy Achiever, some of these people work only four or five hours a day.

Self-employment will not guarantee that you get rich quickly; opportunity does exist to get rich in these fields eventually, however. The self-employed in the United States constitute less than 20 percent of the workers — but some 66 percent of the millionaires. Working for yourself is one of the few ways to generate a lot of wealth through your own efforts and creativity. The key is to truly believe that you deserve to get paid handsomely for your ideas, services, or products as they enhance the lives of people and the state of this world.

Being self-employed or owning your own business can lead to riches, then — but attaining wealth is a bonus and should not be your primary goal in choosing this career path. According to most people who work for themselves, the biggest reward isn't financial. The real big payoff is in the satisfaction you get from having used your intelligence, creativity, motivation, common sense, critical-thinking skills, and risk-taking abilities to develop a successful product or service. There can be no higher thrill or greater satisfaction than having people enthusiastically use your product and service to enhance their lives.

FOR THE TRULY LAZY:

Imagination allows you to think of the journey worth making.

Motivation gets you started.

But patience and perseverance get you there.

More Wisdom for Being a Creative Lazy Achiever:

Perhaps there is only one cardinal sin: impatience. Because of impatience we were driven out of Paradise, because of impatience we cannot return.

— W. H. AUDEN

God Almighty hates a quitter.

— SAMUEL FESSENDEN

Success is not measured by what you accomplish but by the opposition you have encountered, and the courage with which you have maintained the struggle against overwhelming odds.

— ORISON SWETT MARDEN

PAYING YOUR DUES ISN'T EASY, BUT IT'S EASIER THAN NOT PAYING THEM

You may have previously heard a version of this story:

> Two strangers were talking to each other in a local tavern. As is usually the case, the conversation turned to the subject of what they did for a living.
>
> One of the men uttered, "I always wanted to work in a circus. Finally, after two years of trying, I got a job with Bailey's Circus. I enjoy it for the most part; however, it's tough on me. I work fourteen hours a day and only get paid for eight. The pay is only fifteen dollars an hour. I have to wash trucks, sweep floors, take out the garbage, and clean the elephants' pens. One manager keeps telling me he is going to promote me, but he usually yells at me because he thinks I should work a little harder."
>
> The other man replied, "I wouldn't put up with that crap. Why don't you come and work with me? It's a union job, so it's an easy pace. They treat me well, and the starting pay is twenty-five dollars an hour, with double time for overtime — all this for digging ditches!"
>
> Without hesitation, the circus worker responded, "What? Leave show business — to go dig ditches? No way!"

The moral of this story is that you will have to pay your dues if you want to enter any new career field — including show business. Certainly, some success costs too much in effort and anguish and is not worth pursuing. Reality will disappoint you if you believe that everything in life will be easy, however. Enjoy yourself in the present moment as much as possible but realize that there will be difficult times.

Before you make it to where you are comfortably living your dream, you may have to work for a low salary and put up with undesirable tasks and unpleasant conditions. Perhaps you will have to tool around in an old MGB for a few years — like I did — instead of in that new Porsche Turbo convertible. You may even have to work longer hours than you did in the job you gave up. "That's show biz," as they say.

FOR THE TRULY LAZY:

A ll told, the writing is on the wall:

I f you dream about making it big in show
business, it's time to get out of the factory.

O therwise, you will find that the ache of
unfulfilled dreams is the biggest pain you
can ever experience.

More Wisdom for Being a Creative Lazy Achiever:

*You have to know exactly what you want out of your career. If you
want to be a star, you don't bother with other things.*
— MARILYN HORNE

*Where your talents and the needs of the world cross, there lies your
vocation.*
— ARISTOTLE

*People who enjoy the stresses and uncertainties of the starving artist
lifestyle are ultimately the ones who live it and make it.*
— MARK MANSON

At the risk of boring you and also embarrassing myself, I'll share my personal experience, how I had to pay my dues to get where I am today as a writer and self publisher. As is invariably the case when any person achieves a measure of success, some people say I must have been lucky or had some advantage over others.

In fact, I had no advantage over anyone who can think clearly, can write at a ninth-grade level, and is willing to commit to a project. Indeed, when I first started out in this business, I received less respect than comedian Rodney Dangerfield — and remember that Rodney didn't get any!

This goes back to the fall of 1989. I had just published my first book. With one book to my name on how to be more creative, I speculated that I was destined to greatness in the exciting field of professional speaking. In no time, I could be like Brian Tracy or Anthony Robbins, making $20,000 or more per speech. The place to go was Vancouver, B.C. (B.C. stands for bring cash), which had more progressive and innovative organizations than Edmonton, Alberta — or so I thought. I had no doubt that corporations would be lining up for my blockbuster speeches and seminars on creativity.

My move to Vancouver turned out to bring me the best of times and the worst of times. Finally, I could experience a winter away from the frozen, barren tundra known as Edmonton — my hometown. Upon my arrival in Vancouver, however, my financial position was so precarious that I couldn't even afford a nervous breakdown. My apartment was only half-furnished, with stuff the Salvation Army wouldn't accept. My car was a ten-year-old beater — it doubled in value every time I filled it up with gas. A cheap umbrella to deal with the Vancouver rain was my only status symbol.

With a meager income of about $500 a month for teaching a course at Simon Fraser University, $1,000 in savings, $25,000 in student loans, and no seminars coming up in the future, buying a Rolls-Royce and hiring a butler were definitely out of the question — at least for a year or two. In fact, things were getting so desperate that I occasionally thought about asking the buskers and panhandlers on Granville Street for a big handout, before they could ask me for a small one. I certainly wasn't totally nailing it on the success ladder.

FOR THE TRULY LAZY:

Never expect everything to be easy.

If you succeed on the first try, you can be assured that it won't happen again.

Either that, or what you have accomplished is not worth boasting about.

More Wisdom for Being a Creative Lazy Achiever:

He who never sacrificed a present to a future good or a personal to a general one can speak of happiness only as the blind do of colors.

— *OLYMPIA BROWN*

Way too many people are looking for an easy way to achievement, success, and riches. There is no easy way for them. None for you either.

— *LIFE'S SECRET HANDBOOK*

Nonetheless, I tried to keep things in proper and positive perspective. There was a heroic side to my predicament; I was like the starving artist in Paris. Someday, someone would write a blockbuster best-selling book about my suffering and how it made me a stronger person, leading to accomplishments that only the elite of humanity ever attain. Today's severe predicament would be one of tomorrow's most inspirational stories cited in *Success*, *Fortune*, *Entrepreneur*, and *Business Week* magazines.

The eight months that I spent in Vancouver had their good moments. I found adventure and fulfillment in spending time in a different city. To this day, I call Vancouver my second home. Although I didn't have much money, I made a point of going out to dinner and having a glass of wine at a good restaurant at least once a week. I was able to ride my bicycle in relative comfort most days, something I couldn't do in Edmonton because of the cold and snow.

Now for the not-so-good news: After eight months, my finances didn't get any better. Not one seminar or speaking engagement came my way. I escaped an extremely cold Edmonton winter to encounter a Vancouver winter, which was very damp and sometimes almost as cold. In early spring, things really got bad when I couldn't pay my bills anymore. I decided to go home, admitting to others and myself that I was a total failure as a professional speaker and creativity consultant.

Upon my return to Edmonton in mid-April, I was seriously thinking about getting a regular job and hoping it would be on only a temporary basis. I had one seminar booked for May; that was it. My car was barely running. Beans and rice were gourmet to me. I was riding my bicycle, hoping that it wouldn't break down, because I couldn't afford to fix it. Even worse, I was putting up with two obnoxious housemates to help pay the associated costs for the half-duplex that I was renting.

Again, I tried to keep things in proper and positive perspective. I was busted, cleaned out, flat broke, stony broke, bankrupt, insolvent, without a bean, and nonpaying. I was not reduced to poverty, however, nor was I on skid row, nor was I impoverished, nor was I pauperized, nor was I broken, nor was I beggared, nor was I with nothing to hope for, nor was I without prospects.

FOR THE TRULY LAZY:

Have the presence of mind to do nothing when it is right to do nothing.

Often it's best to let things happen instead of trying to make things happen.

Desperation to have something appear is one of best ways to drive it away from you.

More Wisdom for Being a Creative Lazy Achiever:

If we think intelligently about what we can achieve with our time, we can be relaxed, even lazy. In fact, being lazy — having plenty of time to think — may actually be a precondition for achieving a great deal.
— *RICHARD KOCH*

Sometimes it is more important to discover what one cannot do, than what one can.
— *LIN YUTANG*

However beautiful the strategy, you should occasionally look at the results.
— *WINSTON CHURCHILL*

And I was still working at what I most wanted to do — write inspirational books and present seminars on creativity.

Soon after, something magical happened. Call it Divine Intervention, blind luck, synchronicity, or God on your side; sometimes when you need things to go your way, they do. By May, I had managed to get $15,000 worth of seminar bookings for September and October. Was I happy? Happy does not cover it; I was elated. There were no bookings after that until January of the following year — then another $4,500 worth.

Things really improved from then on. By the middle of 1991, I was able to get enough money (even though I had to borrow half of it) to publish *The Joy of Not Working*, which turned out to be my signature book. By following the principles advocated here in this book, I have since been able to earn a decent income on which I live comfortably and from which I have accumulated a net worth approaching $2,000,000 — it was only about $200,000 when the first edition of this book was released in 2002. The important thing is that I enjoy what I do. Better still, I need work only four to five hours a day to experience more freedom and prosperity than most millionaires do in their vocations.

As you pursue your vocational dreams, you will find out — as I did — that creating a life worth living can be difficult at times. You must pay your dues to have a meaningful, fulfilling, and well-paid career. This means you must be totally dedicated to the purpose you have chosen. With anything short of this, you will likely give up at the first sign of trouble.

Zen masters tell us that through suffering we attain the tools for liberation. Although you will experience some pain and discomfort as you try to get established in a new field, the experience itself will not be painful. You will also have good moments. Indeed, something magical will likely happen in your life once you overcome your fears to do something different. As Goethe reportedly advised, "Whatever you think you can do or believe you can do, begin it. Action has magic, grace, and power in it."

When you ask most successful people in the arts and entertainment community how they got to where they are, they will mention a lot of weird coincidences more than they will talk about the suffering they have endured.

FOR THE TRULY LAZY:

Always do the right and honest thing, however more difficult it may appear.

In the long term, it will be the easier and more rewarding thing to have done.

You will be five times worse off if you attain a lot of success tainted by dishonesty and greed than if you attain just a little success.

More Wisdom for Being a Creative Lazy Achiever:

Do not seek dishonest gains: dishonest gains are losses.
— HESIOD

If it lacks integrity, it's not worth pursuing.
Success without integrity — isn't!
— LIFE'S SECRET HANDBOOK

The object of life is not to be on the side of the majority, but to escape finding oneself in the ranks of the insane.
— MARCUS AURELIUS

Some people call these coincidences synchronicity; cynics call them blind luck. Whatever you want to call them — synchronicity or blind luck — you will have a good deal of this experience when you finally move toward following your vocational dreams.

To be sure, paying your dues isn't easy — but it's easier than not paying them. This is the Creative Lazy Achiever's way: find the easiest way possible to achieve satisfaction and happiness. And the easiest way to achieve satisfaction and happiness in the long term is to work at what you are passionate about in the short term.

You will definitely know you are living your dreams and life's purpose when you learn to cope with — and even like — the difficult work, responsibility, tedious tasks, and paying of dues that go with them. Commitment is doing it even if it sucks. Having toughed it out is a way of knowing you deserve to be working in a challenging and rewarding career. The knowledge that you have overcome the odds and become one of the successful in your field will make your success all that more satisfying.

SELLING JUST A BIT OF YOUR SOUL FOR $10,000 TODAY WILL COST YOU MUCH MORE LATER ON

It's impossible to find something illegal, immoral, unethical, or disgusting that people won't do for money today. People will lie to spouses, steal from decent employers, commit burglary, injure innocent people, kidnap helpless children, sell their own children, have sex with strangers, or kill relatives for extra cash.

Some will even consider selling their soul with the expectation of receiving a princely sum for it. Alas: these people haven't thought enough. Apparently many others are also looking for an easier go-around in life and are also ready to part with their souls. With such a surplus on the market, these souls aren't worth all that much.

Oddly enough, Sterling Jones of Fenelon Falls, Ontario, a few years ago tested the market demand for souls by advertising his soul on the Internet

FOR THE TRULY LAZY:

The lust for success and money destroys more character than it should.

Earn your money and success through service to others and not at the expense of others.

When you look in the mirror, you already see the biggest troublemaker in your life.

You don't also want to see a crook.

More Wisdom for Being a Creative Lazy Achiever:

Stand above the crowd even if you have to stand alone. There is no greater way to gain self-respect as well as the respect of other honorable souls in this world.

— LIFE'S SECRET HANDBOOK

To be honest, as the world goes, is to be one man picked out of ten thousand.

— WILLIAM SHAKESPEARE

through auction house eBay. The starting bid was $1.00; the highest bid reached was $20.50. The administrators at eBay eventually halted the sale, saying that Jones had no proof of possessing the merchandise, let alone being able to deliver it.

Many people who can't sell their souls outright think that deception, cheating, and theft are good and expedient alternatives for achieving monetary success. Others commit more serious crimes — such as kidnapping, bodily injury, or murder — to acquire the money they want for an extravagant lifestyle. Indeed, money is the motivator for about 90 percent of all crime committed in North America.

It is understandable that people in less-developed countries, struggling to survive, sometimes resort to petty crime to earn a few dollars. It's harder to accept that so many well-paid people in Western nations will compromise their religious beliefs, values, morals, and ethics to make money. With so much opportunity to earn a decent living in honest ways, it's a sad reflection of our society when businesspeople, lawyers, university professors, and politicians get involved in illegal activities to supplement their already impressive incomes. Western nations have many talented but unscrupulously inclined individuals in desperate need of psychological counseling.

I have often heard the argument that an honest person has no opportunity to become rich in the Western world. This is an untruth fabricated by uninspired, dishonest people. In fact, studies indicate that one of the most important factors for the success of self-made millionaires is their unwavering honesty in their business affairs. Moreover, many disadvantaged people acquire an impressive amount of wealth by working in respectable careers and displaying integrity in all their financial affairs.

Personal integrity is essential to achieving prosperity and financial freedom. Prosperity-conscious people seldom compromise their integrity for money. When they do, it's at a weak moment when they aren't paying attention. They immediately get themselves back on the right track. Creative Lazy Achievers don't sacrifice peace of mind and reputation to earn money in dubious ways. They don't have to resort to dishonesty. Having confidence in

FOR THE TRULY LAZY:

You cannot fake it until you make it; success is not one motivating thought away; a brand new Porsche cannot be brought into being with a kooky affirmation; a flaky prayer cannot ordain a fabulous career; and whispering hope alone will not manifest superb achievement and render remarkable prosperity.

Only the person of integrity, action, passion, commitment, and goodwill carries in his or her heart the capacity for making a big impact in this world and being rewarded appropriately for it.

More Wisdom for Being a Creative Lazy Achiever:

All things will be produced in superior quantity and quality, and with greater ease, when each man works at a single occupation, in accordance with his natural gifts, and at the right moment, without meddling with anything else.

— PLATO

their own abilities, they capitalize on some of the many opportunities available for making an honest and decent living.

When questioned, every one of us would declare that we are honest; yet, each of us has at least a little bit of the crook in us. Everyone is dishonest at one time or another, simply because no one is perfect. Nearly all of us have at one time or another cut a deal with the devil for some additional spending money. Where we draw the line to put ourselves back on the right track determines how much integrity we have.

The best policy is to be as committed to honesty and integrity as we can possibly be, regardless of any opportunities we have to make easy money. Rationally, we may ask ourselves, What harm is there in taking a few moral liberties now and then so we can stiff some sucker for a few bucks? The answer? A great deal of harm may be done in due time.

First, the law of karma should keep us from dishonesty: what we do to others will eventually come back to us in some form or another. With this in mind, we should be committed to total honesty, even when it means our short-term financial position could suffer.

The need to be true to ourselves is also at issue. Values are only worth something when we act rigidly upon them and follow them at all times. This requires that we be as scrupulously honest with all people as we can be. The payoff is peace of mind and the satisfaction that we haven't resorted to cheating or swindling to make money.

Henry Miller observed, "What distinguishes the majority of men from the few is their inability to act according to their beliefs." If your values comprise honesty, integrity, ethics, and decency, it's best to live your life in this manner, regardless of how many of your friends and acquaintances show disrespect for these values.

From the occupational perspective, the best policy is never to get involved in a job, business activity, or other financial endeavor that depends upon a product of dubious value. This applies even if you think that you may be able to make a lot of money at the business. Giving someone the rough end of a business deal may seem like an easy way to pocket some quick cash. Selling

FOR THE TRULY LAZY:

What goes around sooner or later comes around.

As the Buddha says, "Karma means you don't get away with anything."

You get to decide with your actions today whether you will like what comes around sometime in the near future.

More Wisdom for Being a Creative Lazy Achiever:

No cause has he to say his doom is harsh,
Who's made the master of his destiny.
— FRIEDRICH VON SCHILLER

Habits are destiny.
— MASON COOLEY

Enriching others is the only way to get rich, if that is what we desire.
The more we serve, the more we deserve, getting what we give, no
more and no less.
— OLIVER LUKE DELORIE

just a bit of your soul for $10,000 today, however, will cost you much more tomorrow and beyond.

Integrity comes from your character and from how you live your life. Regardless of how much money you make in a dubious business deal, you can't purchase integrity once you have lost it. If you deviate just slightly from being honest, you will be found out sooner or later. Then others will think twice about dealing with you again. What you don't want to lose is the trust of others; such trust is one of the most important factors in maintaining solid professional relationships throughout your lifetime.

It's important to remember the premise that financial satisfaction comes only from making money in a way that is fulfilling to you and beneficial to others. Unless you have a Mafia mentality, being dishonest can't be all that fulfilling — and shafting others can't be beneficial to them. Even if you do make a pile of money, if you lose respect for yourself as well as the respect of others, you will have difficulty enjoying the payoff.

Maintaining your self-respect and personal dignity is essential to achieving success and happiness without putting undue emotional stress on yourself. You don't want to have to face yourself every morning with self doubt. As a Creative Lazy Achiever taking the most relaxed route to success, you must refuse to compromise your integrity for any reason, for anybody, for anything, and for any career.

FOR THE TRULY LAZY:

Enjoy the process of accomplishment without undue expectations of specific outcomes.

The idea that you need a particular outcome at a certain time leads to more trouble than it is worth.

Work toward your goals, but let the universe surprise you with the gifts that come your way.

More Wisdom for Being a Creative Lazy Achiever:

Don't wait to be successful at some future point. Have a successful relationship with the present moment and be fully present in whatever you are doing. That is success.
— ECKHART TOLLE

There is a spiritual realm that encompasses all beings. Make friends with the angels, who will always be with you, although invisible. Make good use of their assistance while following your dreams and in all your creative pursuits through life. Your success and prosperity will come much easier.
— LIFE'S SECRET HANDBOOK

Chapter 3

Your

CREATIVITY

Makes You a

MILLIONAIRE

FOR THE TRULY LAZY:

There are two principles for creative success —
one general and one definitive.

The general principle is that everyone has the
ability to be creative and make a big difference
in this world.

The definitive principle is that almost everyone
has volunteered to be exempt from the general
principle.

More Wisdom for Being a Creative Lazy Achiever:

By nature, men are nearly alike; by practice, they get to be wide apart.
— CONFUCIUS

Creative people. There's just one way to become one: Do something creative.
— SETH GODIN

One is not born a genius, one becomes a genius.
— SIMONE DE BEAUVOIR

THERE'S NO OFF-SWITCH ON YOUR GENIUS MACHINE

The wisdom of all cultures and religions over the ages has stressed the extraordinary power of our thoughts for creating a life worth living. In this regard, all the success we achieve in our lifetime starts with the quality of our thinking, which depends in great measure upon the creativity of our thinking. Indeed, tapping our creativity will do more for our well-being than anything else we do in our lives.

Like the truth, creative thinking can set you free. The more creative your thinking, the less you will have to count on hard work to achieve success. Nothing in this world can pay greater dividends over the long term than imaginative projects. This makes creativity the essence of the Creative Lazy Achiever's lifestyle.

Creativity is a powerful tool for anyone who is willing to put forth the necessary effort to develop it — and use it. Researchers in the area of creativity indicate that the major difference between people who use and people who don't use their creativity is that those who use their creativity simply think they are creative. To put it another way, people who are regularly creative are aware of their natural ability and use it to their advantage.

Make no mistake: you too can develop your creative talent and make it your most important resource for generating wealth, achieving financial independence, and, especially, maintaining emotional well-being. When I come up with a great idea, I say to my friends, "See, there's no off-switch on this genius machine." To maximize the use of your creative mind is to maximize the quality of your life. Once you convince yourself on a deep emotional level that you are indeed creative, you are well on your way to attaining the things you want out of life at a relaxed pace. You can also say to your friends, "See, there's no off-switch on this genius machine."

Here are the seventeen principles of creativity that form the basis of my book *The Joy of Thinking Big*:

FOR THE TRULY LAZY:

Never adopt the excuse that you weren't born as talented or fortunate as others.

The hand that you were dealt at birth isn't as important as what you do with it.

You can always make up in creativity what you lack in talent or good fortune.

Playing the game of life is like playing poker.

Playing three aces badly won't get you as far as playing a terrible hand well.

More Wisdom for Being a Creative Lazy Achiever:

Make good use of bad rubbish.
— ELIZABETH BERESFORD

Ability is the poor man's wealth.
— MATTHEW WREN

- Choose to be creative.
- Look for many solutions.
- Write your ideas down.
- Fully analyze your ideas.
- Identify your problem properly.
- See problems as opportunities.
- Look for the obvious.
- Take risks.
- Dare to be different.
- Be unreasonable.
- Have fun and be foolish.
- Be spontaneous.
- Live the present moment.
- Think way out in left field.
- Challenge rules and assumptions.
- Take your time with major decisions.
- Be patient and persistent.

The way I see it, following these seventeen principles day in and day out can make anyone, including you, much more creative. The degree to which you follow these principles will determine how successful and happy you are in life. This applies whether you are self-employed, run a successful business, or work for someone else.

From a financial point of view, your most valuable asset is not your education, your job, your house, or your bank account. It's your brain. The value you place on your creative mind should be at least a million dollars, because you can use it to generate many times that amount over your lifetime. For this reason, your creativity can make you a millionaire.

Be more creative, and your stash of ideas on how to survive and make money can increase daily. As you build your own collection of ideas on how to earn a living, you will actually start feeling wealthier. Ensure that you record these ideas. I use a visual idea tree to which I add new ideas for books and other

FOR THE TRULY LAZY:

Creativity is your most valuable asset and your best security.

Thus, ensure that you condition your mind more often than you condition your car unless, of course, you value your car more than you do your mind.

Then stick with the car.

More Wisdom for Being a Creative Lazy Achiever:

Creativity varies inversely with the number of cooks involved in the broth.
— *BERNICE FITZ-GIBBON*

The great creative individual . . . is capable of more wisdom and virtue than collective man ever can be.
— *JOHN STUART MILL*

potential moneymaking projects. It's amazing how looking at this collection can pick me up emotionally on a day when things are looking bleak.

The more you see yourself as a creative person, the more prosperous you will feel and the more confident you will be that you can generate a lot more wealth for yourself — without having to work hard for it. This doesn't mean that you should show the world today that you are wealthy by blowing $100,000 on that new Porsche or BMW. That comes later, when you have a million or two stashed away in a savings account.

On the other hand, you shouldn't be inhibited from spending $25 on dinner as you discuss your creative projects with a friend. When you do this, you experience prosperity-consciousness while preparing yourself to enjoy the personal success and wealth that will come your way in the future.

Given that creativity is your biggest asset, it's important that you take better care of it than of any sporty Porsche or BMW. Like an exotic sports car, your creativity is a high-maintenance item. It has to be regularly polished and fine-tuned for you to get the maximum benefit out of it.

You must decide how to use your creativity to get what you want from life. Many good books have been written on how to maintain and enhance your creativity. From a business perspective, Roger von Oech's *A Whack on the Side of the Head* is my favorite. Not only does this book have a great title, but it is fun and easy to read. If you are looking for a more artistic approach to creativity, I highly recommend Julia Cameron's *The Artist's Way*, which can benefit you even if you don't want to pursue an occupation involving the arts. And don't stop after reading one or two books. I try to read every new book on creativity. The more books you read, the more creativity will become your key resource for attaining the things you want at a leisurely pace.

Hubert H. Humphrey declared, "Much of our American progress has been the product of the individual who had an idea; pursued it; fashioned it; tenaciously clung to it against all odds; and then produced it, sold it, and profited from it." This won't change in the future. Individuals working on innovative projects will continue to provide the most benefit to humanity and have the most impressive personal success over the long term.

FOR THE TRULY LAZY:

When starting out in a new field, use your imagination.

To gain credibility, you need to be ten times more creative than the veterans and experts.

Luckily, this isn't all that difficult.

More Wisdom for Being a Creative Lazy Achiever:

We know that the nature of genius is to provide idiots with ideas twenty years later.
— *LOUIS ARAGON*

Your talent and creativity are gifts that the Universe gave to you. The inspirational and magical things that you do with them are the gifts that you give back to the Universe.
— *LIFE'S SECRET HANDBOOK*

THE MORE CREATIVE YOUR THINKING, THE FEWER YOUR CARES AND WORRIES

Remember the major premise of this book: you must think more than the average person in society does if you want to work less and still attain the things you want in life. Thinking more than the average person does won't suffice if your thinking is directed toward the wrong things, however. Your thinking must involve quality thoughts — thoughts that are positive and creative. The more creative your thinking is, the fewer your cares and worries.

Researchers state that the average person thinks about seventy thousand thoughts a day, give or take ten thousand. "Wow!" you may think. "This is pretty amazing. Just imagine the potential of my thoughts if only a small fraction are backed by creative action!" So far, so good — except for two little problems: (1) virtually all of these thoughts are the same ones that the average individual has thought every day for a long, long time, and (2) most of these thoughts are negative, stemming from fear and worry.

Creative ability is wasted due to fear and worry more than to anything else. Some of us who want to write are too afraid that our books will never be accepted for publication. Others with artistic talent go to law school because they fear that their parents don't want them to become actors. Still others with great voices become reluctant accountants because they fear that they couldn't make a living singing.

In the same vein, most people work harder than is required because they are ruled by fear and worry instead of by their creative minds. Fear and worry keep them thinking that the only way they can ensure a reasonable economic future is through dedication to a corporate structure and hard work. As a result, these people live an unbalanced and unfulfilled lifestyle filled with frustration, stress, and disillusionment.

Without doubt, we build positive energy through positive thoughts. Negative thinking — including fear, worry, envy, hatred, and anger — stifles the human spirit and does nothing toward helping us acquire what we want in

FOR THE TRULY LAZY:

Imagine that you are in control of your life.

The question is:

Why do you have to imagine this?

More Wisdom for Being a Creative Lazy Achiever:

Take your life in your own hands, and what happens? A terrible thing: no one to blame.
— ERICA JONG

If your daily life seems poor, do not blame it; blame yourself, tell yourself that you are not poet enough to call forth its riches.
— RAINER MARIA RILKE

If your life is not working, take a hard look at your beliefs and your behaviors. The problem is there somewhere.
— LIFE'S SECRET HANDBOOK

life. We can attain a sense of abundance and a decent income only when we conquer fear and worry with positive thinking.

Some motivational speakers state that you can't afford the luxury of even one negative thought. Avoiding all negative thoughts is probably too much to expect, however; I don't believe that any individual anywhere on Earth can eliminate all negative thoughts. Nonetheless, eliminating most of our negative thoughts can go a long way toward helping us get what we want from life.

Here's a personal example of how I had to use creative and positive thoughts to overcome fear and worry so that I could generate more financial abundance and emotional well-being in my life. Three years before I began writing this book, the sales of my self-published books had gradually declined to levels too low to give me an adequate income. Although I had saved a nice nest egg, I worried regularly about my finances. This went on for a few weeks until I thought about getting a regular job, just to earn money. (In retrospect, I believe that insanity must have had a temporary grip on me.)

To be sure, worrying about my predicament didn't make it go away. Then one day, when I was sitting in a favorite coffee bar with my laptop, I thought back to the years when I had been more than $30,000 in the red and hadn't known how I was going to pay the next month's rent. I also thought about how, back then, I could still go with the flow and write books that eventually generated me a decent income.

Suddenly, I had the revelation that my position in life was pretty good. I had my health. Just as important, I had my creativity. Indeed, these two assets are priceless. With this in mind, I became much more relaxed and positive.

With worry out of the way, I was able to get in touch with my creativity right then in the coffee bar. Within half an hour, I came up with three ideas for new books. To date, two of the books have been published. I set aside the third book, which I still believe offers incredible potential, to write three others, including this one. The uncompleted book was my ace-in-the-hole project in the event I temporarily ran out of great ideas; I have yet to complete it.

It seems strange now, but setting aside worry for half an hour that day was enough to help me turn from a bleak position to one of considerable creative

FOR THE TRULY LAZY:

The way your mind works is sure to affect you.

Think life is easy; or think life is tough.

Either way, you get to be right about it.

More Wisdom for Being a Creative Lazy Achiever:

The law of floatation was not discovered by contemplating the sinking of things.
— THOMAS TROWARD

No pessimist ever discovered the secrets of the stars, or sailed to an uncharted land, or opened a new heaven to the human spirit.
— HELEN KELLER

Reasons only help you sound reasonable. They have nothing to do with manifesting achievement and prosperity in your life.
— LIFE'S SECRET HANDBOOK

and financial opportunity. Only after I was able to put things back in proper perspective was I able to overcome the worry that I was experiencing. This allowed me to return to being a creative, go-with-the-flow author instead of a person ruled by worry and fear.

During the next three years, I worked only two to three hours a day, instead of my standard four to five. I was still able to live comfortably while increasing my savings by another $40,000. Creative action — even for only two or three hours a day — generated me the income. Clearly, continuing to worry about my financial predicament would not have made any positive difference toward adequately rectifying it.

My conclusion from situations like this is that taking a relaxed approach to problems is the easiest way to solve them. Instead of worrying about a predicament, surrendering to it is far more productive. Surrendering to a problem involves accepting it, analyzing it, and then coming up with creative solutions for solving it. Subsequently, the solutions need to be implemented.

To implement creative solutions, we must overcome the fear of what might happen if we fail. We can conquer fear, whether it relates to money or to anything else, only by confronting it head on. Unless put in check, the ghost of fear can grow, unabated, until it is big enough to affect our emotional well-being dramatically and immobilize us completely.

Coming up with creative ideas for earning money or attaining success is difficult when you are worrying most of the time. Moreover, even if you do manage to generate a creative idea or two, ideas produced in such a state will prove to be useless. Undoubtedly, if you worry a lot, you will be too afraid to take risks in implementing ideas, regardless of how remarkable they may be.

Surprisingly, most people think that worrying serves some worthwhile purpose; the opposite is true. The final score on worry is that most (if not all) of it is wasted. At the extreme, worrying makes problems worse in the long term. Clearly, fear and worry won't help you solve problems and achieve your goals in a relaxed manner. Instead, these emotions will drain you of valuable energy and keep you from attaining the desirable things in life that you are capable of attaining.

FOR THE TRULY LAZY:

Any crackpot can come up with a great idea or two.

But that's as far as most great ideas go — they are ideas and no more.

Any amazing idea of yours will always remain amazing in your mind — and absolutely without merit in the real world — as long as you are afraid to do something with it.

More Wisdom for Being a Creative Lazy Achiever:

Words that do not match deeds are not important.
— ERNESTO CHE GUEVARA

The work of the individual still remains the spark that moves mankind ahead even more than teamwork.
— IGOR SIKORSKY

Your real security is yourself. You know you can do it, and they can't ever take that away from you
.— MAE WEST

Excessive worry about problems, and the fear of taking risks to rectify these problems, does not only hinder creativity; ultimately, such worry stifles our goals, hopes, desires, dreams, and prosperity. Worrying about problems is like looking at nasty neighbors through high-powered binoculars. The problems don't disappear; they end up appearing a lot larger — and nastier — than they really are.

SECURITY IS A KIND OF DEATH

One way to overcome the perceived need to work hard is to come to grips with the issue of security. In a world filled with much uncertainty, material wealth is the one thing that is supposed to provide the economic, physical, and emotional security everyone so much desires. Accountants, stockbrokers, financial planners, bankers, and retirement consultants will convince you that building an impressive portfolio of real estate, stocks, bonds, and T-bills is the only way to deal with all this uncertainty.

Security, as traditionally defined, doesn't contribute nearly as much to emotional comfort as most people believe. "No one from the beginning of time has had security," declared Eleanor Roosevelt. What she meant is that security based on materialistic and monetary pursuits is tenuous at best. The superrich can be killed in car accidents and terrorist attacks just as easily as the poor can be. Their health can fail at a much earlier age than that of someone with less money. And most rich people worry about losing their money in the event of a monetary collapse. Weird, isn't it? On one hand, we want and strive for personal security; on the other, there may not be anything that even closely resembles personal security.

To get a better idea of how much security we can get through money, take a hard look at the type of individuals who are most obsessed with security. Security-minded individuals tend to be rigid, unbending, unadaptable, and uncreative. Their expenditures are usually limited to basic food, heat, clothing, and shelter. They won't part with their money even for necessities, unless they know they are getting the best possible deal. Decreasing their bank accounts

FOR THE TRULY LAZY:

A secure life is a sacrificed life.

The person who doesn't do anything risky won't fail much, but the person who does many risky things and fails many times will have made a journey much more worthwhile.

More Wisdom for Being a Creative Lazy Achiever:

If you want a guarantee, buy a toaster.
— *CLINT EASTWOOD*

Adventure may have its risks. Security and routine, however, can be much more injurious to the soul.
— *LIFE'S SECRET HANDBOOK*

I'd rather live precariously in my own office than comfortably in somebody else's.
— *PETER MAYLE*

for a big expenditure brings extreme anxiety, worry, and fear and a sense of vulnerability. Every dollar spent seems to rob them of some inner sense of personal comfort.

To some, security is a steady job with normal work hours, unambiguous activities, strictly defined duties, and a foreseeable future. These people need a steady paycheck and will settle for a regular income with modest increases in pay. They don't realize that holding on to a job does not bring true security. Jobs in modern times aren't as secure as the jobs of just a few years ago. A job may mean security for paying bills today, but when security-minded people lose their jobs, they lose their security, not to mention their identity as well.

It's no wonder that Tennessee Williams declared, "Security is a kind of death." The security-minded individual demonstrates that preoccupation with security is incompatible with living a relaxed, prosperous life. Paradoxically, to feel more secure in this ever-changing world, people must become less concerned with security as defined in the modern-day sense.

You may be surprised to learn that the present-day concept of security is far different from the original meaning of the word. If anyone in this world has security, as originally defined, that security isn't based on money and material possessions. The word *security* comes from the Latin word *securus*, which means "without care." In this regard, true security is an internal state of being, not determined by how much money an individual is able to acquire.

Given the true definition of *security*, the only people who have security are the creative ones who are not obsessed with acquiring as many financial assets as possible. Herein lies the major difference between security-minded individuals and creative, prosperity-minded individuals: when you closely observe human behavior, you notice that the "security"-minded individuals are the most emotionally insecure people on this planet. On the other hand, the least security-minded individuals — the truly creative — are the most emotionally secure.

It's beneficial to look at what makes creative people successful in their own right. The traits of the highly creative are somewhat different from those of the security-conscious. Creative, prosperity-minded individuals thrive on

FOR THE TRULY LAZY:

With due regard to your programmed desire for security, here is something to contemplate:

Security is a great obsession of mediocre minds, but only a passing fancy of great ones.

More Wisdom for Being a Creative Lazy Achiever:

If you aren't living on the edge, you're taking up way too much space.
— *UNKNOWN WISE PERSON*

Beware your desire for security. In another twist of irony from the Universe, living with doubt almost always leads to more achievement and prosperity than living with certainty.
— *LIFE'S SECRET HANDBOOK*

There is no security on this earth. Only opportunity.
— *DOUGLAS MACARTHUR*

ambiguity, dislike nine-to-five routines, question the status quo, and think for themselves in new, exciting ways. In great contrast to security-minded individuals, the prosperity-minded are adventurous, willing to take risks, and willing to undertake projects that are new, different, and challenging. They also want to succeed and be rewarded based on their own merits. Creative people believe in themselves and don't require any advantage over anyone else.

One endearing trait of creative individuals is their flexibility in dealing with the curves that life throws them. Although they don't anticipate catastrophes, as security-minded people do, creative people can handle these situations when they do strike. When adversity strikes, they usually find some opportunity in it. This way, adversity has done half the work for them.

For example, unlike the security-conscious of this world, a creative individual, whose identity is based on interests, values, beliefs, critical-thinking abilities, and imagination, will find an economic downturn a mere inconvenience. Indeed, some highly creative people even find economic downturns to be a great opportunity to do something innovative and constructive for humanity and at the same time to build wealth.

Clearly, to be obsessed with security is to avoid living in the truest sense. You can't have the space for prosperity and success when you are obsessed with security. Financial independence may allow you to do some of the things you would like to do, but unwavering security — physical, emotional, or economic — as a result of having money does not exist. Knowing you have the ability and creativity to earn a living is your best financial security. Keep in mind that security, like success, can be defined in many ways. If you focus less on how much your financial assets are worth and more on what a creative and well-balanced individual you can be, security will take on a new meaning.

No matter how you look at it, creativity is your best security. Your creativity is dynamic, not static like a pile of money or a piece of real estate. Static security is based on some illusion of unlimited protection. Creativity is much harder to lose than is a pile of money or a piece of real estate. You can use your creativity to respond to many different circumstances, yet you will still have all of it intact and available for use in the future.

FOR THE TRULY LAZY:

Here is a myth for you if myths are your pleasure:

There is no more opportunity in this world.

Most people held this false belief fifty years ago; the majority agreed with it five years ago; and practically everyone clings to it today.

Hang on to this myth, and you are destined to miss great opportunities for the rest of your life.

More Wisdom for Being a Creative Lazy Achiever:

When all is said and done, monotony may after all be the best condition for creation.
— MARGARET SACKVILLE

It still holds true that man is most uniquely human when he turns obstacles into opportunities.
— ERIC HOFFER

OPPORTUNITY WILL KNOCK OFTEN IN THE FUTURE: HOW OFTEN WILL YOU BE HOME?

The best investment you can make is to improve your mind's ability to be creative. For creativity to be your biggest money-generating asset, you must take advantage of the opportunities that come your way. "Where are all the opportunities?" you ask. The answer is everywhere, including in your own backyard. One of the great myths that adds to the poverty complex — and keeps many people in poverty — is that all of the good opportunities for making some real money have already been exploited. Every convenience in life — everything you see and touch — was an invisible idea until someone decided to do something concrete with it.

Opportunity drifts in and out of people's lives every day without it being exploited or, for that matter, even seen. Life is full of great opportunities, but people normally inadvertently (or intentionally) ignore them. In this regard, creativity doesn't always entail what no one else sees; it also involves what some see and what everyone is capable of seeing when paying attention. Moreover, creativity entails taking advantage of the great opportunities that others have seen but have neglected to exploit because they were afraid and lacked motivation.

Sadly, most North Americans fail to see a great opportunity even when someone points it out clearly to them. Today's North American is too busy thinking about what sports event to watch on television or what clothes to wear to a party. With all the distractions, most people find it easier to complain that there isn't any opportunity available for today's average person than to pay attention to what is available.

Contrary to popular belief, the financial opportunities available today are unlimited. New careers and businesses are constantly being created. The Internet, with its rapid growth, has generated new types of businesses not even imagined just a few years ago. New products, services, and technologies emerge every day because someone has been creative and motivated enough to take advantage of opportunities.

FOR THE TRULY LAZY:

Don't believe that you have to travel far and wide to discover opportunities.

The best opportunities will always be found in your own backyard, not halfway around the world in someone else's backyard.

You have to look for them, however.

More Wisdom for Being a Creative Lazy Achiever:

Learn to listen intently. Opportunity often knocks softly.
— LIFE'S SECRET HANDBOOK

God hides things by putting them near you.
— RALPH WALDO EMERSON

Make visible what, without you, might perhaps never have been seen.
— ROBERT BRESSON

Furthermore, an unlimited number of problems in today's world offer opportunities for any individual willing to solve those problems. More affordable houses, more efficient heating, more nutritious foods, less polluting cars, better day care, help in cleaning houses, techniques to relieve stress, and less expensive vacations are just a few of the things people need today. Hundreds of thousands of individuals have started highly successful part-time and home-based businesses to meet these needs.

The Western world will continue to offer great opportunities for self-confident individuals willing to risk what it takes to sell ideas, advice, time, products, energy, enthusiasm, and services to those who need them. In the last ten years, more millionaires have been created in the United States than were created in the previous two hundred years. The next ten years will probably see ten times as many millionaires created as exist today.

Even if you don't want to be a millionaire, but just want to earn a decent living in a fulfilling way, you must spot and capitalize on the many opportunities that the world has to offer. You must ignore those people who say it can't be done. Some of the greatest opportunities can be found in things that other people say are impossible. In fact, greater opportunity often exists in the things that people say can't be done than in the things that they say can be done. When you achieve what at one time was unthinkable to you, you will be in your glory. The satisfaction you experience will be even greater if others have said you couldn't do it.

To take advantage of opportunities, you must be prepared for them when they appear. The way to prepare for them is to keep your biggest asset in great shape. Your creativity is the cornerstone of all your money-making ideas, so it's important that you use it regularly. In a mystical way, when you prepare yourself for opportunities, more opportunities will come your way.

If you want to be a Creative Lazy Achiever making a difference in this world, you must be able to spot the opportunities around you and to do something productive with them. Undoubtedly, that opportunity will knock often in the future. The question is, How often will you be home?

FOR THE TRULY LAZY:

Having a great deal of opportunity proves nothing.

Opportunity without creative action is like a brand-new Ferrari without an engine.

You possess something valuable, but it won't get you anywhere.

More Wisdom for Being a Creative Lazy Achiever:

The ability to convert ideas to things is the secret of outward success.
— HENRY WARD BEECHER

Don't ever keep a great opportunity waiting.
— LIFE'S SECRET HANDBOOK

True creativity often starts where language ends.
— ARTHUR KOESTLER

CREATIVE LOAFING IS GOOD FOR YOUR CASH FLOW

Years ago, Henry Ford hired an efficiency expert to examine the performance of the Ford Motor Company. The expert presented a highly favorable report, except that he regarded one employee with great suspicion. The expert told Henry Ford, "That lazy man over in that office is wasting your money. Every time I go by that office he's just there sitting with his feet on his desk."

Henry Ford replied, "That man once had an idea that saved us millions of dollars." Ford added, "At the time he had the idea, his feet were planted right where they are now — on that same desk."

The moral of this story is that you must relax and use your imagination if you want to come up with the blockbuster idea that is going to save your company millions of dollars or earn you a cool million or two. Creative loafing, or productive relaxation, if you may, is actually good for your cash flow. Just one good session of creative thinking can be worth an extra million dollars to you sometime in the future.

Sadly, a large number of us today desperately want something different in our lives. We find neither the time nor the space to generate the ideas that would contribute to a better lifestyle in the future, however. We are too preoccupied with the drudgery of our everyday lives to sit back and do some relaxed creative thinking.

Inasmuch as we live in a work-oriented society, most of us feel that we must be continually busy to be successful. We are led to believe that fabulous wealth and fame await the person who works the hardest. Indeed, we fear that taking it easy will prevent us from obtaining even a small measure of wealth. The irony is that taking it easy now and then would help us achieve wealth a lot sooner. Contrarily, overwork can be hazardous to our creative ability.

The work ethic is an insidious force in our society; it dictates that we must always be busy doing something constructive if we are to be considered productive members of society. Many people think loafing is an evil activity

FOR THE TRULY LAZY:

You can wind up poor in the midst of economic opportunity and prosperity.

Or you can create riches in the midst of economic decline and chaos.

It depends on how you orchestrate your spirit and your soul.

More Wisdom for Being a Creative Lazy Achiever:

Experience your uncertain ventures with a good measure of glee. To be delighted while on the rocky road to success and prosperity is not generally understood by less adventurous souls. They will think that you are crazy. This is the fun part!

— LIFE'S SECRET HANDBOOK

Read, every day, something no one else is reading. Think, every day, something no one else is thinking. Do, every day, something no one else would be silly enough to do. It is bad for the mind to continually be part of unanimity.

— CHRISTOPHER MORLEY

that stifles ambition and interferes with productivity. On the contrary, loafing can be a sign of ambition. It makes some individuals much more productive — and much wealthier in the long run than those won't-ever-make-it workaholics.

Many highly creative people have been productive because they were able to goof off and indulge in constructive loafing. Mark Twain did most of his writing in bed. Samuel Johnson rarely rose before noon. Other Creative Lazy Achievers considered to be notorious layabouts include Oscar Wilde, Bertrand Russell, and W. Somerset Maugham. Marc Allen, owner of publishing company New World Library, has been lazy all his life and is very prosperous.

Like most people in Western society, you have probably been programmed to be hardworking, straight and narrow, and analytical. You may thus have difficulty accepting that you can benefit from intentionally being a slacker on a regular basis.

To be highly creative, experience prosperity-consciousness, and work toward financial independence, you must be able to sit back, ponder the big picture, and take the long-term view. Certain conditions and attitudes tend to support the generation of new and blockbuster moneymaking ideas more than do others. The best environment for generating a bigger cash flow over the long term, while also preparing for financial independence, is relaxed and has few distractions.

Many of the great achievements in the history of humankind started with great insights in a relaxed setting. Archimedes was having a bath when he came up with the displacement theory. Sir Isaac Newton was sitting under a tree when an apple hit him and he had his insight about gravity. These two renowned individuals probably would not have come up with their respective discoveries while in a modern workplace setting. Sitting at a desk, answering the phone, checking email, and frantically churning out paperwork all day doesn't stimulate the imagination.

Perhaps you have found that most of your creative ideas come to you at a time other than when you are frantically trying to complete a project. Again, creative loafing is important to your prosperity. A busy lifestyle will keep you from tapping into the creative ideas that could be worth a fortune. When you

FOR THE TRULY LAZY:

A lways reserve enough time in your day to loaf, relax, and think creative thoughts.

T his will have much more effect on your financial and personal well-being than two or three hours of extra work:

More Wisdom for Being a Creative Lazy Achiever:

Idleness is an appendix to nobility.
— *ROBERT BURTON*

A good rest is half the work.
— *YUGOSLAV PROVERB*

He lacks much who has no aptitude for idleness.
— *LOUISE BEEBE WILDER*

In an industrial society which confuses work and productivity, the necessity of producing has always been an enemy of the desire to create.
— *RAOUL VANEIGEM*

utilize the entire potential of your creativity, you can be somewhat lazy and still wind up a lot richer than the highly stressed Workaholic of Western society.

Billionaire Nicolas Hayek, cofounder and chief executive officer of Switzerland's Swatch Group, had to be productive to reshape the insolvent Swiss watch industry back into a multibillion-dollar empire. Hayek advises, "Do schedule your time, but never schedule 100 percent of it. You'll kill your creative impulse if you do."

Even U.S. presidents must indulge in some creative loafing to be effective in their jobs, according to Ellen Simons of the Newhouse News Service. Simons wrote that the most effective U.S. presidents had been nappers and not Workaholics. She reached this conclusion based on conversations with people who have conducted research in this area.

Historians told Simons that hard work and brains have not guaranteed success among U.S. presidents. According to these historians, Dwight Eisenhower and Calvin Coolidge, who took time for rest and relaxation, were much more effective than Jimmy Carter and Teddy Roosevelt, who were continuously busy and worked late into the night. Princeton University history professor James McPherson concluded that the most effective presidents have been those who delegated effectively, made major decisions when called upon, and didn't work all that hard.

Blockbuster ideas come when you feel at ease, free from strain or tension, and confident about yourself. Creative loafing is therefore one of the best ways to unblock your creative spirit. Creative loafing is also for individuals who want to find ways to get to know themselves, others, and the world better, instead of constantly being busy with no real payoffs.

If you aren't spending at least one or two hours a day in activities that can be deemed as creative loafing, you aren't doing as much as you can to create the lifestyle you want in the future. The more intensely you work, the more you need creative loafing as an important resource to help you develop great income-generating ideas. Hiking in the woods, walking in the park, or riding a horse in the meadow all will give your mind a chance to relax and wander into new and exciting territory.

FOR THE TRULY LAZY:

Strive for originality in thought and action.

Be first; be different; and be daring.

Only then will you make a significant difference in this world.

You may even attain greatness.

More Wisdom for Being a Creative Lazy Achiever:

The radical invents the views. When he has worn them out the conservative adopts them.

— *MARK TWAIN*

Imagination is the voice of daring. If there is anything Godlike about God it is that. He dared to imagine everything.

— *HENRY MILLER*

Not only does loafing kindle your imagination to greater heights; it's good for your long-term health, because it reduces stress and helps prevent many diseases. Moreover, when you loaf, you are preparing for the time when you will achieve enough wealth to take it easy. You are giving yourself a taste of the freedom and prosperity that are coming to you.

One of the most productive things you can do is to take a week or two to vacation away from home and your workplace and generate ideas for putting your talents and knowledge to better use. The income-producing ideas will be a big step toward your continued prosperity and wealth building. The intent is to concentrate on opportunities for three or four hours a day and forget everything else related to your workplace. Don't worry about the income you lose while you are away. The ideas you generate will be worth a hundred times what you sacrifice by being away from work.

Keep in mind that you don't have to be a millionaire to take a few days off here and there. I have been doing this all my adult life, even when I was more than $30,000 in debt. Taking time off hasn't prevented me from getting out of debt and creating some wealth for myself. In fact, my creative loafing has helped me to better evaluate my ability and potential so that I could find an occupation that suited my desired lifestyle. Consequently, I don't have to succumb today to the frenzied and stressed-out lives that most people in Western nations lead.

An unexpected day off from work provides an opportunity to reflect on life and let your mind wander in all directions. This can pay big dividends — psychological, physical, and financial. Your immediate payoff won't be in the numbers of hours worked and in how much money you have earned. Instead, the return on your investment will be in interesting thoughts and great ideas that you can put to use to earn more money in the future.

All things considered, hard work is the enemy of creativity. The more hard work you indulge in, the less creative you become. Only when you have plenty of time to loaf and to think wildly will you be creative and come up with the great ideas that make the world a better place and that will earn you a comfortable living in the process.

FOR THE TRULY LAZY:

J ust one great idea can change your life dramatically.

L ook for it.

I t's there somewhere.

More Wisdom for Being a Creative Lazy Achiever:

Foster a curiosity for the uncommon, regardless of how unpopular it is. The uncommon is where opportunity likes to hide.
— LIFE'S SECRET HANDBOOK

An idea, when coupled with action, can indeed be a very powerful force.
— ROBERT J. RINGER

The fishing is best where the fewest go, and the collective insecurity of the world makes it easy for people to hit home runs while everyone is aiming for base hits.
— TIMOTHY FERRIS

Chapter 4

ACCEPT THE TRUTH

about Money and You

Won't Have to

WORK SO HARD

FOR THE TRULY LAZY:

Money is what you make it.

Depending upon who you are — and your frame of mind — money can be anything you want it to be.

Money can be the root of all evil, or that which answers all things, or something that burns a hole in your pocket, or a means to freedom, or an interesting concept — or even a stupid concept!

More Wisdom for Being a Creative Lazy Achiever:

The universal regard for money is the one hopeful fact in our civilization. Money is the most important thing in the world. It represents health, strength, honor, generosity and beauty. . . . Not the least of its virtues is that it destroys basic people as certainly as it fortifies and dignifies noble people.

— GEORGE BERNARD SHAW

MONEY DOESN'T TALK; IT WHISPERS

Money. Money. Money. Practically everyone aspires to having many piles of money. Clearly, nothing else in the Western world is perceived to be as precious as money.

Money touches every area of our lives to some degree. The amount of money we have at our disposal can affect the quality of our relationships, friendships, housing, leisure, and health. If we use our imaginations, we can think of an unlimited number of ways in which we can use money to add comfort and pleasure to our lives.

Yet for all its wondrous implications, money can be terribly disappointing. This directly contradicts a basic axiom that guides nearly all human behavior — the axiom that the more money we have, the happier we will be.

Sadly, people who have excessive designs on bettering their financial positions allow themselves to be manipulated, humiliated, and degraded while in the pursuit of money. Moreover, unrealistic expectations for what money can do for them lead them to experience the negative emotions of envy, deprivation, dejection, and disillusionment. Still worse, the pursuit of wealth eventually costs many people their lives. They forget how to relax, how to laugh, and how to enjoy themselves — even if they do acquire wealth.

Perhaps you are thinking by now that I am trying to convince you to forget about earning more money. Not at all! That is not my intention. As much as anyone else, I enjoy earning money and spending it on things that enhance my life. I am not about to suggest that you give up the idea.

Above all, this chapter is intended to put money in its place so that you have realistic expectations about what a great amount of money can do for you. If you need less money in your life, you won't have to work as much and as hard for it. Like the Costa Rican fisherman cited in the opening story in chapter 1, you can still experience a full, relaxed, satisfying, and happy life.

To most people in Western countries, a large amount of money is deemed an essential ingredient for happiness. For this reason, it's important that money

FOR THE TRULY LAZY:

So what is money to you?

Take some time to create your own special definition.

This will put you in better touch with money.

Whatever your answer, congratulations!

According to Zen masters, you are neither right nor wrong.

Again, money is what you make it.

More Wisdom for Being a Creative Lazy Achiever:

Money makes the world go around — that and other stupid cliches.
— UNKNOWN WISE PERSON

and its relationship to happiness be put in proper perspective. Money is an important element for comfort and enjoyment of the finer things in life, but how much money people need to be happy is another question.

Money may eliminate certain modes of unhappiness, but it certainly won't guarantee true happiness — even for a day. No one agrees with this more than University of Illinois psychologist Edward Diener, who specializes in research regarding what makes people happy. After conducting many studies, Diener has shown that money can add pleasure to people's lives, but it won't bring the true happiness that comes with self-respect, accomplishment, and satisfaction.

Money can do a lot for us, but we allow it to have too much control over our lives. The problem is that most of us don't acknowledge the truth about money. Some of us may not know the truth, and we don't want to hear it. Some of us know the truth deep down, but are in denial about it.

Most of us cling dearly to our beliefs, attitudes, and assumptions about money regardless of how much contradictory evidence the world brings our way. Accepting the truth would destroy the fantasy that acquiring a lot of money will save us. Denying the truth about money keeps us locked into an unhealthy relationship with it and impedes our enjoyment of life.

Although our relationship with money changes as our circumstances and personal outlook change, we don't spend enough time contemplating the true value of money. Money can take on a different meaning when we think about it from a more spiritual or Zen perspective. After we ponder money in new ways, we may even find that many aspects of it are absurd.

Perhaps you have really been broke at some time. I am not talking about a time when you considered selling the cabin cruiser or the cottage to help you through a downturn in the economy as you continued to bask in relative luxury. I am referring to a trying situation when you were so broke that you may not be able to think of a word or phrase to describe it. "Hard up" or "short of funds" just wouldn't do.

If you have experienced this mode or broke, you undoubtedly had a special connection to money at that time. "When the well's dry," declared Benjamin Franklin, "we know the value of water." When unemployed and busted, you

FOR THE TRULY LAZY:

Whatever value you place on money, you must take responsibility for it.

If money is evil to you, you created it being evil; if money is a problem to you, you created it being a problem; and if money is joy to you, you created this concept.

Take responsibility for your concepts.

And be clear that these are just concepts — nothing more and nothing less.

More Wisdom for Being a Creative Lazy Achiever:

Poverty of goods is easily cured; poverty of soul, impossible.
— *MICHEL DE MONTAIGNE*

We often buy money very much too dear.
— *WILLIAM MAKEPEACE THACKERAY*

think about money and what it can do for you quite differently than when you have a job to help you obtain life's great pleasures.

If you have been truly broke, undoubtedly you have imagined that you would be really happy when you could elevate yourself to the financial position that you enjoy today. Your happiness today, however, is probably far from what you imagined it would be. Perhaps your happiness hasn't increased a bit, despite the fact that your wealth has increased considerably. You may even be more unhappy and more miserable now that you have greater wealth.

Unfortunately, acquiring more money alone does not lead to an overall improvement in our lives. Life is never that easy. Obtaining a substantial amount of money doesn't necessarily mean enhancing the quality of all parts of our lives.

Many impending matters in life cannot be solved with money, regardless of how wealthy we are. In many cases, indeed, having more money keeps us from having the things that are important to us. After we have paid for the necessities of life, trying to acquire more money is likely to do just as much harm as good.

Most of us know deep down that money doesn't buy happiness, but we don't want to believe it. Yet we need only look to see the many unhappy people living at the higher socioeconomic levels. Many wealthy people don't appear to be any happier than people of modest means. These wealthy people don't laugh more, don't jump for joy more, and aren't any more blown away by life.

In fact, rich people rarely experience the happiness and prosperity that are supposed to come with wealth. They may be wealthy by all rational measures, but their state of happiness indicates quite the opposite. A study by University of Illinois research psychologist Ed Diener showed that one-third of the richest people in the United States are not actually as happy as the average-income person in this country. Moreover, J. Paul Getty and Howard Hughes — both well-known billionaires — reportedly became more miserable and unhappy the more their riches increased.

It shouldn't be surprising that some of the most miserable and unhappy individuals we meet are wealthy people. Some people become more miserable

FOR THE TRULY LAZY:

L ook closely around you.

Y ou will see many people with a lot less money than you; yet some of these people will be much happier than you.

Y our thoughts may be, "I am sane; therefore, these people must be crazy."

M aybe — maybe not!

P erhaps it's the other way around.

More Wisdom for Being a Creative Lazy Achiever:

If money is your hope for independence, you will never have it. The only real security that a man can have in this world is a reserve of knowledge, experience, and ability.

— HENRY FORD

and unhappy as they become wealthier because of their high expectations for what money can do for them. Originally, these people think that acquiring a great deal of money will make them happy. It doesn't — and then they have no excuse for being unhappy, so they become even more miserable and unhappy.

Should you have the misfortune of being unhappy, and should you be looking to money to change your life, it's time for a reality check. Once and for all time, you are unhappy because you don't have your emotional act together. Don't feel bad about it — just do something to rectify the situation. We all fall into that trap at one time or another. Unless we address our shortcomings in this area, we are destined to be unhappy, even if we end up in the highest socioeconomic group in our country.

Clearly, a lack of money for basic necessities will leave us unhappy and dissatisfied about our position in life. This doesn't mean that having a lot of money will leave us truly happy and satisfied, however. Money may get us to a neutral state, somewhere between unhappy and happy, somewhere between dissatisfied and satisfied. Generally speaking, however, more money coming into our lives won't get us beyond that neutral state. After we reach the neutral state, happiness depends on things that money can't buy.

Money can be a vehicle for enjoying life to its fullest, provided you take the time and effort to get a good grasp on what money can and can't do for you. Riches will enhance your life if you have a healthy attitude toward money and detract from it if you don't. Put another way, understanding what money can do for you can help you get what you want from life. In the same vein, knowing what money can't do for you can save you a lot of disappointment, dissatisfaction, disillusionment, ulcers, and nervous twitching.

It's important that you view wealth as a means to an end instead of as a measurement of your worth as an individual. Ironically, the less you evaluate your self-worth based on money, the more freedom you give yourself to be creative and the more wealth you are capable of generating in the long term.

In a materialistic world, prosperity is invariably associated with hoards of money and countless possessions. The Creative Lazy Achiever's prosperity, however, is prosperity in its original sense. Indeed, *prosperity* comes from the

FOR THE TRULY LAZY:

Believe it or not, money can't buy happiness.

No, this isn't a strange joke.

Believe that money can buy happiness — and the joke's on you.

More Wisdom for Being a Creative Lazy Achiever:

If you believe that money can buy happiness, then why don't you try selling some of yours?
— THE LAZY PERSON'S GUIDE TO HAPPINESS

There's nothing wrong with working diligently for money and the many good things money can buy. Ensure in your pursuit of money, however, that you haven't lost the priceless elements of happiness that money can't buy. There are many.
— LIFE'S SECRET HANDBOOK

Latin word *spes*, which means "hope and vigor." To the Creative Lazy Achiever, being truly prosperous means being positive and happy in the moment, regardless of level of conventional success.

The feeling of prosperity is an emotional state available to you whenever you want it. It has little to do with your wealth or the economy. You can experience prosperity-consciousness in a bad economy, even though many well-off people experience poverty-consciousness in a booming economy. The rich may get richer and the poor may get poorer, but you don't have to do either to feel prosperous.

MONEY SOLVES ALL PROBLEMS — EXCEPT ALL THOSE THAT IT DOESN'T SOLVE

Even if we completely accept that money won't bring true happiness, most of us dream about having a million dollars or two lying around. This is not just because of the pleasure, comfort, and style that money can provide. We expect something magical. We have the notion that money will take care of our problems. Unfortunately, the more we cling to this notion, the more we fool ourselves. If we do become rich, reality intrudes to put money in its place, especially in regard to problems.

Like it or not — and based on my observation, most people don't — you will have to face both minor and serious problems all your life. This is true no matter how emotionally stable you become, no matter how much money you earn. Many people look to riches to eliminate at least their major problems, if not their minor ones. Clearly, reality dictates that money solves all problems — except all those that it doesn't solve. And many of the problems that money doesn't solve are major.

Reuters some time ago reported on the plight of then thirty-one-year-old Gary Coleman, former star of the 1970s comedy *Diff'rent Strokes*, who at one time had a net worth of $18 million. After encountering medical bills, lawsuits with his parents, disputes with his managers, and a series of dead-end jobs, Coleman hosted the Gary Coleman Celebrity Web-a-Thon in an attempt to

FOR THE TRULY LAZY:

Priceless things that are the foundations of happiness cannot be bought.

These include peace of mind, satisfaction, and self-worth.

So why are you trying to acquire a lot of wealth in the hope of buying these things?

More Wisdom for Being a Creative Lazy Achiever:

The things that are most precious to the human soul are those that are beyond price — integrity, true friendship, health, achievement, reputation, true courage, great character, gratitude, greatness, emotional stability, common sense, self-esteem, creativity, wisdom, spiritual fulfillment, and peace of mind. These can't be rented, bought, or sold — regardless of how much money you acquire.
— LIFE'S SECRET HANDBOOK

If you want to feel rich, just count all the things you have that money can't buy.
— UNKNOWN WISE PERSON

bring himself out of bankruptcy. Absurd as it seems, the Internet telethon included a phone-sex line with Coleman talking dirty to unsuspecting listeners. Even $18 million wasn't enough to eliminate Coleman's major problems — both financial and personal. Indeed, having to deal with a large sum of money at one point in his life seems to have created many new problems for him.

But let's address the problems that money can solve. If you are able to handle money, more money can solve your financial problems. The degree to which you are able to handle money at any level of income will determine how many major financial difficulties you will have throughout your lifetime.

If you have financial problems with a modest income, you will probably have financial problems just as serious with an income double or triple what you earn today, unless you change your ways.

Minimizing your money problems is crucial if you are to have the time and energy to pursue the things that make you happy. The choices you make in all areas of your life — such as where you choose to live — will determine whether you have financial difficulties. These choices will depend upon how much you earn, how much you spend, your expectations for the good life, the influences of your spouse and children, your self-esteem, any envy you feel, and your need for perfection. The extent to which you choose well in these areas will determine whether you have financial problems.

Your ideals are to be healthy and to be free of any overriding personal problems. You must always be prepared for difficulties, however. Contrary to popular belief, your problems won't end once you join the jet-setting moneyed class. Financial bliss doesn't eliminate personal problems. You will experience troubles regardless of how rich or talented you become. You can only hope they won't be as serious as Gary Coleman's.

The bad news regarding money and problems has just a bit more to it. Through an extensive study conducted in the 1990s, Ed Diener, the University of Illinois psychologist specializing in happiness and money, found that people who end up with a lot more money actually end up with more problems. Extra income creates difficulties for people who have more money than they require for basic needs and desires.

FOR THE TRULY LAZY:

This is difficult for most people to grasp:

Money doesn't talk; it just whispers.

A large of amount of money solves all problems — except for all those it doesn't solve.

And for the biggest disbelievers, money tends to create a few really big problems that weren't there before.

More Wisdom for Being a Creative Lazy Achiever:

Prosperity has no power over adversity.
— PUBLILIUS SYRUS

The only incurable troubles of the rich are the troubles that money can't cure.
— OGDEN NASH

Here are some of the difficulties these people might experience:

- Relationships with friends and acquaintances suffer.
- Individuals may be alienated from their peer group.
- Monitoring finances becomes more troublesome and time-consuming.
- Looking after possessions requires more time and energy.
- Fear of theft of property and money becomes more acute.
- Fear of losing money in investments increases.
- Life becomes more complicated in general.

Stanley Goldstein put a proper perspective on money and its relationship to problems. "If you want to hear about the power and glory of wealth," he declared, "ask a man who's seeking it. But if you want to learn of wealth's burdens and difficulties, ask a man who's been wealthy a long time."

It's best to forget the idea of a problem-free life. Multimillionaire status doesn't allow you to move into an exclusive complex called Paradise Palace where you experience Nirvana into eternity. Indeed, you may become a multimillionaire by following the Creative Lazy Achiever's philosophy. In doing so, you will have attained a great sense of satisfaction and happiness from your accomplishments. This will be a result of having to deal with problems — not of not having to deal with them.

Based on the evidence, you need to be good at handling problems if you earn more money, inherit some, or win a major lottery. "The bigger the problem, the better," should be your motto. Clearly, being really good at handling major personal and financial problems as a poor person is prerequisite to handling major problems as someone who is rich. Self-made millionaires are extremely competent in dealing with all sorts of problems. That's how they got their wealth in the first place.

FOR THE TRULY LAZY:

M oney is neither good nor evil.

T here is nothing wrong with having a lot of
money.

J ust don't expect it to guarantee contentment
and peace of mind.

T he less happiness you expect to get from
money, the more benefit you will be able to
get from it.

More Wisdom For Being a Creative Lazy Achiever:

*Wage slaves may live in big houses. They might drive Porsches. It
doesn't matter how "rich" you look, if you can't walk away from your
job — even for a second — because you would no longer be able to
pay the bills, you're a wage slave.*

— SARA GLAKAS

FINANCIAL INSANITY HAS ITS OWN BIG FOLLOWING — INCLUDING YOU AND ME

It's a lot easier to avoid trouble than to get out of trouble. Yet most of us go to great extremes to invite trouble into our lives. Mishandling money is one of our favorite ways to get ourselves into difficulty. We seem easily to forget that each spending choice we make determines how much money we need in our lives and how much we have to work for.

Unfortunately, money is more often misused and abused than it is used intelligently. Most people haven't figured out how to use money wisely to truly enhance their lives. Most, it seems, act rationally with their money only when they can't dream up any more irrational ways to spend it. To be sure, financial insanity has developed its own big following — including you and me.

The problem is that our spending habits do not reflect our deepest values and desires. We waste our funds on questionable material possessions at the expense of things that we cherish, such as freedom and financial independence. We may save meticulously for a sabbatical or retirement, for example, but then, after a year or two, blow the entire $10,000 that we saved in a moment of weakness on a new stereo system — which we hardly use, because we don't have time for it. Alternatively, we may buy a new wardrobe that will be out of fashion in just one season.

In this day and age, here are the two main reasons that so many people are in debt big time and struggling to make it from pay check to pay check:

1. Instant gratification takes much too long.
2. A need is any luxury that the neighbor happens to possess.

If you believe that you are over and above irrational behavior with money, you are probably in denial about the issue. Perhaps a strange and confusing relationship exists between how hard you work to earn your money and how easily you spend it at times. You may pinch pennies when buying food at the market on payday, but later blow what's left on gadgets that you could easily do without.

FOR THE TRULY LAZY:

An old Italian proverb advises, "Make money your devoted servant; otherwise, it will be an overbearing master."

In other words, learn to control money, or it will control you.

More Wisdom for Being a Creative Lazy Achiever:

If you make money your god, it will plague you like the devil.
— HENRY FIELDING

You are not your money, therefore let it serve you, not you serve it.
— RON SMOTHERMAN

If you can't enjoy spending money with the same degree of satisfaction that you experience while earning it, then your prosperity consciousness needs some serious work.
— LIFE'S SECRET HANDBOOK

In fact, many people spend most of their paychecks on the best junk money can buy. Worse, they tend to buy this junk with money they haven't yet earned. Will Rogers stated it well: "Too many people spend money they haven't earned, to buy things they don't want, to impress people they don't like." Although we don't want to admit it, each of us exhibits at least a little bit of this insanity.

Money, unfortunately, brings out the eccentricity in each of us. An occasional quirk or peculiarity in our spending habits is normal. But consistent irrational behavior with money is detrimental to our personal and financial well-being. We end up working long and hard hours to earn money but don't experience much happiness and satisfaction from the things we buy.

Indeed, modifying serious irrational monetary behavior requires effort; otherwise financial problems will continue to interfere with our leading a happy and fulfilling life. At the source, most irrational financial behavior is not really about money at all. Financial behavior goes deeper than money itself.

Emotional shortfalls and a poor sense of reality are generally unconscious motivators of our irrational monetary behavior. Through money we channel our deeper wants, needs, goals, hopes, and dreams. Behind every irrational spending urge is a profound emotional need that requires attention. That need can be for power, status, fame, freedom, revenge, respect, security, or self-respect. It can even be for love.

Not just one but several unfulfilled emotional needs often drive us to purchase things that we really don't need or that we can't afford. We must be able to deal with these needs head-on, because in most cases, the purchase won't make things better. The only way to change irrational financial behavior is to get in touch with our underlying emotional needs and then to fulfill those needs in ways that money can't. Ultimately, these needs can be satisfied only through our outer creative efforts and through inner mental gymnastics.

FOR THE TRULY LAZY:

If you are feeling unhappy even though your friends consider you to be well-off, you don't need more money.

What you gravely need is more creative spirit in your soul.

You may also need a whack on the side of the head from a Zen master.

More Wisdom for Being a Creative Lazy Achiever:

More than enough is too much.
— UNKNOWN WISE PERSON

Nothing is enough to the man for whom enough is too little.
— EPICURUS

To be without some of the things you want is an indispensable part of happiness.
— BERTRAND RUSSELL

YOUR BEST PURCHASES WILL TURN OUT TO BE THE ONES THAT YOU NEVER MADE

For Creative Lazy Achievers, the most important factor for attaining financial success at a relaxed pace is to have money under control. This requires that you spend less money than you earn. Evaluating why you spend money on whatever you spend it on is a good place to start.

The key is to consult your feelings when a spending urge presents itself. Ask yourself what psychological need you are trying to satisfy or emotional shortfall you are trying to fill by buying something new. You could be looking for self-respect, the respect of others, ego, approval, belonging, security, power, sense of community, structure, purpose, prestige, reward, status, peace, happiness, or love, or you could be trying to combat an envy of others or a fear of being disliked.

Once you have identified the psychological needs that require attention, tell yourself the truth about what you will get in return for the money that you intend to spend on these items. If you are honest with yourself, you will admit that most purchases won't make any significant positive impact on satisfying emotional needs. Possessing the object only complicates your life by getting you further into debt and taking up more of your valuable time.

Miguel de Cervantes advised, "Make it thy business to know thyself, which is the most difficult lesson in the world." Knowing yourself and what drives you to spend your money — whether it's cars, homes, fashions, or cool stuff — is essential to having total control of your finances. It can be the difference between having a million dollars for retirement and having nothing.

More often than not, things that people purchase impulsively end up giving them little pleasure and don't enhance their lives in any way. Just a little thought can prevent this from happening to you. If you always question the true value of every service or item you purchase, your purchases will go down dramatically as have my purchases because of my continual self-questioning.

FOR THE TRULY LAZY:

Devote just a few moments of clear-headed thought before you buy anything.

Always ask yourself how much satisfaction you will get in return for your money.

Your best purchases will turn out to be the ones that you never made.

More Wisdom for Being a Creative Lazy Achiever:

He who buys what he does not need steals from himself.
— UNKNOWN WISE PERSON

Unhappiness is not knowing what we want and killing ourselves to get it.
— DON HEROLD

A man is rich in proportion to the number of things he can afford to let alone.
— HENRY DAVID THOREAU

This technique requires that you ask questions about every intended purchase to be absolutely clear whether it serves a real need or a true personal want. By meticulously asking questions, you will find that you don't really need or want most of the things that capture your interest. Besides building wealth, you will enjoy life more when you stop wasting time and money on things that don't bring you pleasure and satisfaction.

It's important that you confront your innermost feelings about the benefit a purchase will bring you. You must have a sense of what you will get in return for your money. Do you want the object of your expenditure just so you can keep up with a friend who has purchased something similar? Are you considering purchasing the object because you feel lousy about something and you think the object will make you feel better about yourself?

For your spending decision to be rational, you must be certain that you value the product. The more you savor the product, the more rewarding your spending decision will be. Ensure that you make your decision according to your own needs and not according to what someone else has advised. Relax. Tell the truth about whether you will get pleasure and satisfaction from the item you are purchasing. Only then can you make purchasing decisions based on critical analysis instead of on purely emotional impulses.

You must also be honest with yourself about whether you can afford whatever you are considering purchasing. The best test is whether you have the cash on hand. Is the cash designated for something else, or is it surplus specifically for these types of purchases?

If you have to buy an item on credit when you are already having a hard time paying your bills, the item will probably do you more harm than good. This applies even to something that means a lot to you. The product won't bring you much pleasure if you worry all day and at night trying to figure out how to pay for it. I can't overemphasize the need to consider every purchase you think about to avoid buying things that won't enhance your life. Don't forget about the small expenditures — the $20 CD here, the $4 cappuccino there. In the words of Benjamin Franklin, "Beware of little expenses; a small leak will sink a great ship."

FOR THE TRULY LAZY:

When you want something badly, work at giving up your desire for it.

You will find that not wanting something is as good as having it.

And it's a lot less trouble.

More Wisdom for Being a Creative Lazy Achiever:

There is often less danger in the things we fear than in the things we desire.
— JOHN CHURTON COLLINS

I should be suspicious of what I want.
— RUMI

You can't have everything; where would you put it?
— STEVEN WRIGHT

Small expenses can downgrade your financial position from a surplus to a deficit in no time. This is no way to attain financial independence. Keep in mind that the difference between spending 10 percent more than you earn versus spending 10 percent less than you earn is, respectively, the difference between financial chaos and imminent personal bankruptcy versus financial satisfaction and personal financial freedom.

Forcing yourself to become fully aware about every intended purchase may seem tedious, but the trouble will be worth it. Saving money doesn't have to come at the expense of enjoying yourself in the present. On the contrary, you can probably enjoy your present moments more when you know that you have a nice nest egg available for contingencies and for enjoying life's pleasures in the future.

If this chapter influences you to ponder and decide against just one major purchase, you will have received a return of several hundred percent on your investment in this book. Don't stop there, however. Getting in touch with the emotional quirks that drive your irrational spending can save you hundreds of thousands of dollars over the next decade or two. This means that you will have to work only half as hard as the general population to lead a full, relaxed, happy, and satisfying life.

THERE'S MORE TO LIFE THAN HAVING IT ALL

"We almost made it but we wanted it all." This line from Burt Bachrach and Carole Bayer Sager's song "We Wanted It All" typifies most North Americans in the twenty-first century. These people will never quite make it to the destination called happiness, because they want to have it all — fame, a lot of money, a big house, a beach cabin, two or three cars, an attractive spouse, three model children, a nanny, great friends, and increasingly exotic vacations.

The have-it-all mentality is a powerful and insidious force in Western society today. Advertisers have convinced many people that not only are they entitled to every imaginable luxury, but they deserve it as well. Most people's

FOR THE TRULY LAZY:

Money will be your friend — like all friends — only if you treat it with respect.

Treat it with disrespect, and you will always have financial difficulties, regardless of how much money you make.

More Wisdom for Being a Creative Lazy Achiever:

People who don't respect money don't have any.
— J. PAUL GETTY

To understand money you must lighten yourself by dropping your belief systems about money. Until you are willing to get off your positions and consider the possibility that you might not be right in what you believe about money, money will continue to be a problem for you.
— RON SMOTHERMAN

If you borrow money to make money, you've done something magical. On the other hand, if you go into debt to pay your bills or buy something you want but don't need, you've done something stupid. Stupid and short-sighted and ultimately life-changing for the worse.
— SETH GODIN

expectations are so high, in fact, that even God would have a hard time providing them with everything they would like. Oddly enough, although the middle and upper classes today have more than their respective counterparts of any other generation, research indicates that their satisfaction is on the decrease. If anything has led to a lower degree of satisfaction, it's the have-it-all mentality.

Ultimately, the have-it-all mentality won't bring more happiness and satisfaction. How can it? In the quest to have it all, people work far too much to enjoy the things that they do acquire. Sadly, they never stop to figure out that one of the greatest time wasters — and life wasters — is their insatiable desire.

Not only does the have-it-all mentality deprive people of time to lead a balanced lifestyle, it leaves them financially challenged. Because of overspending, fully 65 percent of Canadians claim that they are "barely getting by." In the same vein, people in approximately 20 percent of the households in the United States with more than $100,000 in income per year claim that they spend nearly all of their money on what they perceive as "basic necessities." (I am sure that this brings tears to the eyes of people in households with $45,000 a year who still manage to save 10 to 20 percent of their income.)

People who suffer from the want-it-all syndrome get themselves into a vicious work-and-spend cycle from which they cannot break free. They buy things, work to pay for them, buy more things, work longer and harder to pay for them, then buy even more expensive things, and on it goes. Hoping for a raise to solve financial problems never works. When a big raise comes, it soon goes into possessions that are supposed to be newer, bigger, glitzier, prettier, or more fun.

Wanting to have it all carries a huge emotional price. The desire for newer and bigger possessions and the fear of not having them rule people's lives more than they admit. These people live in denial about how their spending habits are connected to their feelings of inadequacy as human beings. Seeing people with more and better stuff than they have further fuels these inadequacies. These people will always feel inadequate because they will always find others who have more and nicer possessions than they have.

FOR THE TRULY LAZY:

Why waste so much time, energy, and money trying to buy the biggest house that your credit rating will allow?

In truth, a small house can hold as much happiness as a large one.

Sometimes it will hold even more.

More Wisdom for Being a Creative Lazy Achiever:

I suppose I passed it a hundred times,
But I always stop for a minute.
The house with nobody in it.
— JOYCE KILMER

Home is any four walls that enclose the right person.
— HELEN ROWLAND

American writer Maurice Sendak once remarked that there must be more to life than having it all. Indeed, Sendak was right. If more of us contemplated how much is enough in our lives, a lot more people in this world would be happy and satisfied. In our quest to have it all, we end up experiencing less peace, happiness, and satisfaction than we would if we learned how to be satisfied with much less.

To get our finances and lifestyle in order, the real challenge is to decide what possessions are important to us and to disregard the rest. The question really has to do with what we need versus what we want. We must know where to draw the line between "must haves" and "would like to haves." Most of the apparent must-haves — in reality, things that we don't need at all — demand way too much of our time, energy, and money.

Understand that you have few actual needs. You are a creation mainly of wants and of only a few needs. With a little critical thought, you can transfer most of what you have listed as needs to nothing more than wants.

In fact, upon close observation, you will find that every necessity has already been provided for you all of your life. Think about it! All your necessities have always been provided; otherwise, you would be dead! In his 2018 book titled *This Is Marketing*, marketing guru Seth Godin pretty much agreed when he stated, "What we need is air, water, health, and a roof over our heads. Pretty much everything else is a want."

Your mind may be your greatest asset, but remember: it can play tricks on you as well. The most common trick it plays is in making you believe that you need all the things you buy. If you allow it to keep playing that nasty trick, it can cost you your money, your health, your individuality, your self-esteem, and your sanity. Indeed, it can cost you a full, relaxed, happy, and satisfying life.

If you do not hold your wants in check, you will never have enough money to buy the things you truly desire and the freedom to pursue the Creative Lazy Achiever's lifestyle. This is the final score when it comes to wanting it all: If you expect to have it all, you will have nothing. If you learn to be happy with nothing, however, you will have it all. To be sure, you can only have it all when you live in the moment and appreciate what you already possess.

FOR THE TRULY LAZY:

No special talent is required for you to master money.

Just earn your money before you spend it.

Follow this simple principle, and you will have fewer financial difficulties than the vast majority of humankind.

You will also show maturity that most adults fail to achieve throughout their entire lives.

More Wisdom for Being a Creative Lazy Achiever:

Money is easy to handle. There are two secrets: The first is to spend less than you make. If this doesn't work for you, then the second one is definitely for you: Make more than you spend. That's all there is to handling money.

— HOW TO RETIRE HAPPY, WILD, AND FREE

Chapter 5

You Have

THE MONEY

but Can You

BUY SOME TIME?

FOR THE TRULY LAZY:

Don't make your life goal to make the most money that you can.

Instead, make your life goal to make the most you can out of life, regardless of how much money you make.

More Wisdom for Being a Creative Lazy Achiever:

Life shouldn't be printed on dollar bills.
— CLIFFORD ODETS

If I had known what it would be like to have it all, I might have been willing to settle for less.
— LILY TOMLIN

When money is lost, little is lost;
When time is lost, much more is lost;
When health is lost, practically everything is gone;
And when creative spirit is lost, there is nothing left.
— LIFE'S SECRET HANDBOOK

BEING SUCCESSFUL AT WORK IS IRRELEVANT IF YOU ARE A FAILURE AT HOME

One of the realities of modern life is that we all have many things we would like to pursue but limited time for pursuing them. We have to make decisions as to how we spend our time, not only in how much we work, but also in how we utilize our leisure time. Irrespective of our income and net worth, we can be truly prosperous only if we have a great balance between work and play. For a great work-life balance, we work forty hours or less a week and don't feel time-deprived in our personal lives.

Clearly, being successful at work is irrelevant if you are a failure at home. It's possible to be a huge success at work and to miss out on life completely. You shouldn't sacrifice present happiness for a few extra bucks, especially if only to spend the money frivolously on gadgets that won't enhance your life significantly. Day-to-day life will have little meaning if your main reason for going to work is to pay for the things you don't have time to use.

What's the point of being well-off financially if you have no time to truly live, but only exist? Rest and constructive leisure activities are half of what you need for a life of purpose and accomplishment. Friends, family, adventure, walking, meditating, creative loafing, and spiritual fulfillment — not working long and hard hours — are the things that make live worth living.

If you find yourself focusing on business and financial issues to the detriment and exclusion of everything else, you have a clear case of poverty-consciousness. Money and possessions are important to a certain extent, but not important enough to be put ahead of everything else.

If you are leading an unhealthy lifestyle to earn big money, you are poor no matter how you much earn. You won't be prosperous until you sleep enough, eat well, exercise regularly, and spend time with friends and family. Not surprisingly, researchers have found that individuals who find the time to do the things they enjoy are much happier and live longer than people who plod through their work and regular routines at the expense of personal life.

FOR THE TRULY LAZY:

Consider this carefully:

If you work more than eight hours a day, you are in the wrong job.

Either that — or you are doing it wrong.

More Wisdom for Being a Creative Lazy Achiever:

The man who does not betake himself at once and desperately to sawing is called a loafer, though he may be knocking at the doors of heaven all the while.

— HENRY DAVID THOREAU

The truth inherent in Parkinson's First Law: Work expands to fill the time available for its completion. Once you've mentally absorbed this reality, and cultivated the habit of guarding against it, you've practically bought yourself a whole new life.

— ROBERT J. RINGER

The richest people in the world are those who have fun earning their living and at the same time have a healthy work-life balance. I believe in erring on the side of having a good time at the expense of my work. Because my career is so enjoyable, I have probably blurred the line between work and play as well as anyone can. Nonetheless, I wouldn't imagine working more than an average of four or five hours a day on my projects.

You could argue that extracurricular play is not important if you enjoy your work; work then becomes play. I disagree with this argument, simply because this world offers so much in the way of excitement, adventure, and learning. To confine yourself to a world of work is to miss out on many of life's other rewarding experiences. If you don't enjoy your work and you look at it primarily as a means to meet financial obligations, finding the right balance between work and play is even more crucial for your contentment.

Success in experiencing the deeper meaning in life is very different from success as defined in the modern world. Financial success is shallow if fulfillment, virtue, and true happiness are missing. Many people today are successful in that they are materially wealthy, but they don't have any real purpose and meaning. This is partly because they don't create the time to pursue a more holistic and spiritual lifestyle. The consequences are frustration, stress, and burnout leading to bad nerves, twitching, strokes, and heart attacks.

Many people immersed in a life of overwork take refuge in visions of a full, relaxed, satisfying, and happy life sometime later, when they will be able to slow down and enjoy themselves. They are waiting for the day when they finally acquire a sufficient sum of money, or the day when they retire on Social Security, to really start living. Unfortunately, this day rarely comes. People either die first or don't have the capacity to enjoy themselves when they eventually have enough money and time.

In fact, if we think that we don't have enough time for constructive leisure, we won't have. It's easy to be busy just to be busy. It's easy to fill our lives with activities and then complain about the time crunch. Whenever we do have some spare time, it's easy to lie on the couch and watch TV for two or three hours, then complain that we don't have time for more meaningful leisure

FOR THE TRULY LAZY:

Everything in life has a price attached to it.

There is a price for not working hard enough — and there can be an even larger price for working too hard!

More Wisdom for Being a Creative Lazy Achiever:

The cost of a thing is the amount of what I will call life which is required to be exchanged for it, immediately or in the long run.
— HENRY DAVID THOREAU

The real price of everything, what everything really costs to the man who wants to acquire it, is the toil and trouble of acquiring it.
— ADAM SMITH

Don't overdo things that shouldn't be done in the first place.
— UNKNOWN WISE PERSON

activities. It takes intelligence and courage to slow down, be ourselves, and do some real living.

Above all, individuals with an excellent work-life balance have set their priorities right. In order to have such an excellent work-life balance, you must prioritize your needs and wants and then focus your time and energy where they make the most difference. Start by ranking the following life challenges according to importance in your life: spouse, kids, health, personal growth, job, community, spiritual fulfillment, and education.

Only you can decide whether you have your priorities right and are living according to them. You must be completely clear about the type and quality of life you want to live. The degree to which you put time and effort into the things that really matter will determine your overall happiness and satisfaction.

It is possible to have a lifestyle that coincides with your deepest values if you really want it. Taking control of your life starts with you — not with your employer, the government, your spouse, society, or anyone else. You can choose whether you want to opt out of excessive work and materialism for a life that includes more leisure activities, time to relax, more time with your kids, and more rewarding work.

Making life-altering changes to balance your lifestyle isn't easy, but millions have shown it to be possible. They've gotten their emotional acts together and accomplished what the majority have not. These successful people live happier and fuller lives, spend more time with their families, connect with nature and the community, and enjoy the many simple pleasures that they had forgotten in their pursuit of the good life. And even if only 2 percent in the western world can lead such a full, relaxed, happy, and satisfying life, you can choose to be in this group. It's a matter of paying the price.

Regardless of what you and others believe, the system does not enslave people; people themselves do so. If you do not accept this, you will have given your creative power away. Denial will prevent you from making the changes that can really affect the quality of your life. After you have set aside all of your excuses, the first step is to explore how you can change your lifestyle — if you have a lifestyle to begin with, that is.

FOR THE TRULY LAZY:

Know the moment when to work diligently.

Even more important, know the moment when not to work, but instead to relax and play.

This not only will benefit you immensely, but also will astonish your friends and colleagues.

More Wisdom for Being a Creative Lazy Achiever:

But lo! men have become the tools of their tools.
— HENRY DAVID THOREAU

Yet it is in our idleness, in our dreams, that the submerged truth sometimes comes to the top.
— VIRGINIA WOOLF

Sometimes it's important to work for that pot of gold. But other times it's essential to take time off and to make sure that your most important decision in the day simply consists of choosing which color to slide down on the rainbow.
— DOUGLAS PAGELS

TO WORK IS HUMAN, TO LOAF DIVINE

In the nineteenth century, when asked to give a lecture for a large fee, Swiss naturalist Jean Louis Rodolphe Agassiz replied, "I cannot afford to waste my time making money." It's too bad that few people today have the same priorities. The world would be a better place if we did. To be sure, the nature of modern society dictates that we work to earn a living. When we overdo earning a living, though, we suffer the loss of a relaxed, satisfying, and prosperous lifestyle.

Consciously or otherwise, most people accept the formula for leading satisfying, worthwhile, and successful lives that is espoused by corporations, educational institutions, the media, and advertisers. Few stop to think why they are doing what everyone else is doing. Most of those who do think are afraid to do something different, even if they desperately want to.

When it comes to earning a living and having a good life, the majority of people think that the single most important thing to do is to work hard. These people are wrong, what they need, in fact, is to learn how not to work hard. Learned workaholism is difficult to give up because its practice provides a perverse form of gratification. Moreover, the Protestant work ethic has influenced us to believe that working hard is virtuous regardless of the results we attain.

Although you may have been hardworking all your life, you can transform yourself into a lazy, intelligent, and productive person all at the same time. Hardworking — and hardheaded — individuals focus on the number of hours they put in; you must focus on results. The difference can be remarkable in terms of the income you make and the balanced lifestyle you are able to lead.

To adopt a more relaxed approach to earning a living, we must be constantly alert so that the hardheaded people who say it can't be done don't influence us. For example, Stephen M. Pollan in his book *Live Rich* advises his readers: "Making money is hard work. You have to wake up earlier, work harder all day long, and go to sleep later than everyone else. The only ways to

FOR THE TRULY LAZY:

Most people are too busy working on insignificant projects and pursuing life's frivolities to tap their creative abilities.

It's a mistake to be one of them.

Striving for excellence where excellence doesn't matter is the stuff that misfits are made of.

More Wisdom for Being a Creative Lazy Achiever:

Little things affect little minds.
— BENJAMIN DISRAELI

Anyone can do any amount of work provided it isn't the work he is supposed to be doing at that moment.
— ROBERT BENCHLEY

Success is important only to the extent that it puts one in a position to do more things one likes to do.
— SARAH CALDWELL

make money without hard work are to inherit it and to win the lottery." By following this advice, we will find, inevitably and tragically, that hard work leads to inferior results.

An alternative to Pollan's advice is a much more positive and prosperous approach to making a good living and having a great life. We can adopt and follow the premise of self-made millionaires such as Robert Ringer, author of *Million Dollar Habits*, and Robert T. Kiyosaki, author of *Rich Dad, Poor Dad*. They advise that, provided you make your mind your greatest asset, money is not that difficult to obtain. And provided you save and invest a good portion of what you obtain, it is not that difficult to multiply. In other words, it is not hard work but creativity and astute investing that lead to high monetary results.

The foundation of this book is that you must think more and work less than the average person in society to enhance the overall quality of your life. For optimum results, you must challenge your values about work and leisure. Seventeenth-century French writer and moralist Francois, Duc de La Rochefoucald wisely declared, "The greatest gift is the power to estimate correctly the value of things."

Therein lies the root of the problem. Most people aren't able to correctly value work. Indeed, they overvalue work and undervalue leisure. This is the result of years of programming by religious organizations, educational institutions, corporations, society, and advertisers.

The life-work issue can't be addressed until work is put into its proper place. Although work has many positive benefits, people tend to ignore just as many harmful effects. Thus, the words of William Faulkner: "One of the saddest things is that the only thing that a man can do for eight hours a day, day after day, is work. You can't eat eight hours a day nor drink for eight hours a day nor make love for eight hours — all you can do for eight hours is work. Which is the reason why man makes himself and everybody else so miserable and unhappy."

Contrary to popular belief, work hasn't always been held in such high regard as it is today. The early Greek philosophers, such as Plato and Aristotle, declared that total leisure was the ultimate richness. Pursuing wealth, power,

FOR THE TRULY LAZY:

Here is something else to consider carefully:

To work is human; to loaf divine.

More Wisdom for Being a Creative Lazy Achiever:

My father taught me to work, but not love it. I never did like to work, and I don't deny it. I'd rather read, tell stories, crack jokes, talk, laugh — anything but work.

— ABRAHAM LINCOLN

Ours is a culture based on excess, on overproduction; the result is a steady loss of sharpness in our sensory experience. All the conditions of modern life — its material plenitude, its sheer crowdedness — conjoin to dull our sensory faculties.

— SUSAN SONTAG

Work is the refuge of people who have nothing better to do.

— OSCAR WILDE

and status through work was a form of voluntary slavery that failed to enhance the human condition. Plato and Aristotle were critical of people who kept working after they had satisfied their basic needs. They concluded that these people were working and pursuing luxury and power in an attempt to cover up their fear of freedom.

Moreover, Plato and Aristotle did not associate leisure with idleness and slothfulness as many people do today. They viewed leisure as an activity on a much higher level than work. Plato described leisure as "activity, not passiveness, a mind and body in action, not frozen contemplation." In other words, leisure time was an opportunity for human beings to exercise their minds, bodies, and spirituality in new, exciting, and satisfying ways not to be experienced in the workplace.

Another popular belief today is that it is natural for human beings to work long and hard hours. This belief is far from the truth. Working long hours is a recent bad habit initiated during the Industrial Revolution.

Anthropologists tell us that peasants in medieval Europe, irrespective of how poor they were, actually worked much less than we do nowadays. Leisure time in ancient Greece and Rome was much more plentiful than what we have today, for example. Nearly a third of the year (109 days out of 355) was designated as inappropriate for working or business purposes.

Also, in the few remaining primitive societies today, people work less than people in industrialized societies do. Men in the Sandwich Islands of Hawaii work only four hours a day. Similarly, aborigines in Australia work only as hard as they have to for their necessities. To the surprise of many in industrialized countries, people in these societies lead happy and fulfilling lives and have fewer wants than people in the rest of the world.

As in ancient Greece, a meaningful and prosperous life today shouldn't be based only on satisfying work and the accumulation of material possessions; it also requires challenging and rewarding leisure activities, including some that develop the mind, body, and soul. Most people today can attain a more holistic approach to life — one that integrates the material with the non-material — if they really want it. Unfortunately, few people do what is required to attain it.

FOR THE TRULY LAZY:

THE CREATIVE LAZY ACHIEVER'S MOTTO

Regardless of how little time and work someone takes to perform a task, there has to be a more efficient and effective way to perform it.

More Wisdom for Being a Creative Lazy Achiever:

If there's a harder way of doing something, someone will find it.
— RALPH E. ROSS

Hard work pays off in the future. Laziness pays off now.
— UNKNOWN WISE PERSON

It is in vain that you rise up early and go late to rest, eating the bread of anxious toil for he gives to his beloved sleep.
— NEW TESTAMENT, PSALM 127:2

Contrary to what work-crazed individuals believe, you don't have to work hard for fifty or sixty hours a week to enjoy yourself sometime in the future. One of the greatest dangers of adopting the workaholic lifestyle is the possibility of sacrificing your present-day happiness for twenty or thirty years only to get hit by a bus just before you are able to retire and enjoy life. Then you will be both dead and hardheaded.

BUSYNESS IS THE LAST REFUGE OF UNPRODUCTIVE AND UNFULFILLED PEOPLE

Perhaps you are like millions of people in today's world whose need to make a living has gotten out of hand and become an obsession. You yearn for more excitement, more adventure, more satisfaction, more happiness, and an overall higher quality of life. You never find the time for these things, however. If this is your situation, you are probably a Workaholic or close to being one. If you admit that you have a small problem with overwork, the problem is likely much bigger than you would like to acknowledge.

Given that society and most corporations support the workaholic mentality, it's easy to understand why so many people are Workaholics. Unfortunately, the workaholic lifestyle fails to deliver on substance and fulfillment. This situation is pathetic; a recent study concluded that tens of millions of workers are dissatisfied with the balance between their careers and their personal lives. Indeed, half of all employed people between the ages of twenty-five and forty-four work so many hours that they don't have sufficient time to spend with their friends and family.

Many of these people work long hours, take few vacations, and tie their identities to the workplace. Instead of having friends, family, and church satisfy their emotional needs, they rely on their bosses and colleagues at work. Sadly, work has become their primary source of self-esteem, recognition, and outer approval.

Therapists today see more and more patients who have lost their true selves in their work. Maynard Brusman, a San Francisco-based consulting

FOR THE TRULY LAZY:

You are fooling yourself whenever you think you are productive just because you have worked fourteen hours in a day.

You will be truly productive when you do the same amount of work in four hours and take the other ten hours to enjoy the good things life has to offer.

More Wisdom for Being a Creative Lazy Achiever:

The successful people are the ones who can think up things for the rest of the world to keep busy at.
— DON MARQUIS

No matter how rich you become, how famous or powerful, when you die the size of your funeral will still pretty much depend on the weather.
— MICHAEL PRITCHARD

psychologist, recently told *Fast Company* magazine, "The workplace has become their community center — where they work out, get a massage, go to parties. They come to me anxious, and they don't know why. They've become caught up in the culture. The question is, Is that healthy? From what I've seen, it isn't."

Regardless of how much you may be in denial about it, sooner or later your well-being will suffer if you continually work too hard. As you work harder and harder, you will begin to look pathetic. The more dedicated you are to your job, the more you will maintain this appearance. Physical and mental fatigue will become normal.

With time, things will get even worse. Too much work, like too much exercise, will leave you with nothing in reserve. Health researchers have learned that overwork eventually leads to ailments such as ulcers, back problems, insomnia, depression, and heart attacks. Any of these can take all of your energy in no time. For good measure, you can add an early death to this list, even if a bus doesn't hit you.

When your life is out of balance, you fly with only one wing. A balanced life depends upon a balanced state of mind. It requires emotional investments, not only financial ones. To the extent that you transform your most cherished beliefs about work and your approach to it, you can transform your life beyond your wildest dreams.

Above all, you must not allow yourself to think that workaholism is some intelligent and heroic state, even though at least 20 percent of the working population is addicted to work. Perfectionism, compulsiveness, and obsessiveness all complement the Workaholic mentality. Because Workaholics invest 100 percent of themselves in their jobs, they have nothing left for friends, family, and themselves. Some psychologists go so far as to say that severe workaholism is a symptom of a disorder of the mind that leads to spiritual emptiness.

Sadly, many Workaholics abstain from social and leisure activities because they don't know what to do with themselves outside of work. This applies even if they are married and have children. Indeed, sociologist Arlie Hochschild,

FOR THE TRULY LAZY:

Regardless of how much you like your work, it's dangerous to have your occupation become your life.

If your identity is your work, you will have no identity at all when you lose your job or retire.

Not a great result, is it?

More Wisdom for Being a Creative Lazy Achiever:

They intoxicate themselves with work so they won't see how they really are.
— ALDOUS HUXLEY

When you learn to let go of the mundane and the ordinary, the extraordinary will start being part of your life.
— LIFE'S SECRET HANDBOOK

author of *The Time Bind: When Work Becomes Home and Home Becomes Work*, concludes that many dual-income couples spend long days at work, not because their employers want them to, but because they want to escape the turmoil of family life. Some of these domestic and social misfits have even been known to come to work whenever they are sick, just to escape family life.

Truth be known, Workaholics are not strong individuals; rather, they are weak individuals who don't have the will to enjoy life more. Health and happiness seem unimportant to them. People overwork to avoid their inner growth, the experience of fun, their families, social outings, and themselves. Workaholics are also poverty-conscious individuals who lack confidence in their abilities. Otherwise, they wouldn't spend so much time working.

No matter which way you look at it, salvation from a meaningless personal life can't ever be found in the workplace. Work should be a part of daily living, but not more important than family activities, exercise, solitude, and play. You must not put all of your energy into a job; you must learn to experience and appreciate leisure activities as well. Tapping into your leisure-related passions and talents early in life will make your professional life, as well as your retirement life later on, much richer and more satisfying. That's what I have done even though I had to get fired from my Engineering job to do it.

To overcome your obsession with hard work, you must reject society's judgments regarding your role as a dedicated consumer supporting the economy and as a decent person based on how hard you work. If you can make a good living by working four hours a day, do it — and forget about everyone else! Create your own definition of success, and develop a strong sense of independence from your coworkers.

The key is never to allow others to pressure you into working the same hours they work. Tell your colleagues and supervisors that you are too productive and prosperous to work more than eight hours a day. If your eight hours are productive, you are not obligated to work overtime just because others are doing so. A good manager will know how valuable you are to the company and will respect you for having the self-confidence and self-respect to choose to live a balanced life.

FOR THE TRULY LAZY:

Understand that Workaholics aren't productive people.

Quite the contrary.

A Workaholic is someone who takes twice as much time to accomplish half as much as a Creative Lazy Achiever.

More Wisdom for Being a Creative Lazy Achiever:

There are only four types of officer. First, there are the lazy stupid ones. Leave them alone, they do no harm. Second, there are the hard-working intelligent ones. They make excellent staff officers, ensuring that every detail is properly considered. Third, there are the hard-working, stupid ones. These people are a menace and must be fired at once. They create irrelevant work for everyone. Finally, there are the intelligent lazy ones. They are suited for the highest office.

— GENERAL VON MANSTEIN ABOUT GERMAN OFFICERS

Lest you think that I am some hypocrite advising you to do something that I wouldn't have the guts to do myself, let me assure you that this is not the case. Several years ago, I was an instructor at a private vocational school when I received a disturbing memo. From that point on, it stated, all instructors were to arrive at 8:00 A.M. and remain at the institution until 5:00 P.M.

I immediately decided that I wasn't going to abide by this directive. I had been hired on the basis of having the freedom to come and go as I chose, provided I taught the classes at the specified times. My freedom and personal life were too important for me to spend nine hours each day at work, even if none of the other instructors had the courage to make an issue of the directive.

The following day, a supervisor confronted me as I was leaving for the day. "Leaving already, Ernie?" he asked. "It's only three o'clock." I replied, "Yes, Joe, as a matter of fact, I am. I am much too prosperous to work past three o'clock. How about you?" While the supervisor struggled to come up with an answer, I exited the building on my merry way to some relaxation and real social contact at one of my favorite coffee hangouts.

Because I had the highest student evaluations of all the instructors at the vocational school, no supervisor ever again questioned me about the time of my departures. The supervisor who confronted me was also an instructor but received extremely poor ratings from the students. Although he put in long hours at work, this didn't translate into excellence in the classroom. This shouldn't be a surprise; workplaces are filled with Workaholics who work twelve or fourteen hours a day, yet they produce much less than those who work six, seven, or eight hours.

This brings up another important trait of most Workaholics: most are unproductive workers. In fact, work is the best thing ever invented to help them kill time. Workaholics may be constantly busy, but so what?

Work, even if it is tedious and boring, is the Workaholics' savior. Often Workaholics use busyness as an escape from something important. Some people stay busy at the workplace to avoid important family responsibilities or social life. Similarly, people are often too busy to get fit and healthy. Taking longer than necessary to complete tasks, either consciously or subconsciously,

FOR THE TRULY LAZY:

This may surprise you:

You can get more done by doing less.

The key is to put your efforts in the right places and leave them there.

More Wisdom for Being a Creative Lazy Achiever:

One principal reason why men are so often useless is that they divide and shift their attention among a multiplicity of objects and pursuits.
— *G. EMMONS*

Do the right things instead of trying to do everything right.
— *PETER DRUCKER*

I didn't have time to write a short letter, so I wrote a long one instead.
— *MARK TWAIN*

is an effective way to avoid putting in the time and effort to exercise and enhance overall well-being.

Unorthodox as it may seem, busyness is the last refuge of ineffective and unproductive people. Creative loafing and other constructive leisure activities take initiative and imaginative thinking, whereas busyness in most jobs requires little initiative and virtually no creative thinking. The Workaholic finds it much easier to perform work duties laid out by someone else than to find the energy and creativity to pursue the activities that could add balance to his or her life.

If Workaholics had satisfying personal lives that provided purpose, identity, and a sense of community, they wouldn't have to invest their heart and soul in the workplace. Moreover, if they were more creative, they wouldn't have to spend so much time earning a good living, because they would be more productive. Taking time off would help them enjoy life much more. It would also make them even more productive at work.

Busyness is one of those bad habits sanctioned by organizations, educational institutions, and the media. Indeed, in today's society, if you're not extremely busy and stressed out, you're not considered important. Mainstream society fails to consider that being busy and being productive are two entirely different things.

Being busy doesn't lead to success. If it did, a lot more Americans would feel more successful, and fewer would be short on time. The key is to be effective, not to be busy. The biggest money makers in any company are always the creative people who know how to do things in an unorthodox manner. They realize that longer hours don't translate into higher productivity. Moreover, they realize that great wisdom is needed to avoid many work activities. In other words, they operate with 3C Vision — and not with 3D Vision as do the Workaholics of this world.

FOR THE TRULY LAZY:

You must be clear about what really counts, and you must be even clearer about what doesn't count.

Only then can you make something great out of what matters most — and make nothing out of what matters least.

More Wisdom for Being a Creative Lazy Achiever:

Refuse to be intimidated by the adage, "Anything worth doing is worth doing well." This is one of the most ridiculous statements ever made. The truth is, most things worth doing aren't worth your best efforts. There are just a few really important things that are worth doing well. After that, a greater number of things are worth doing adequately. Even more things are worth doing just haphazardly enough to get by. Of course, most things aren't worth doing at all — best left for the misfits of this world to pursue.

— BENJAMIN A. SLOAN

MOST THINGS WORTH DOING AREN'T WORTH YOUR BEST EFFORTS

Clearly, the things not worth doing at all are the worst time wasters in our lives. Most people are busy with tasks that are minimally relevant to leading a productive, fulfilling, and happy life. These people claim that they are time-deprived, yet they watch three hours of TV a day. At work, they search the Internet, make four or five personal phone calls, and socialize with their colleagues. Then, at the end of the day, they complain when they have to work two or three hours past quitting time.

Lack of time is not the problem; the problem is how we handle time. People who are the most productive and prosperous are those who invest their time in a few important activities and pursue them at a comfortable rate. They use their time efficiently and differently. To the Creative Lazy Achiever, or to any peak performer, focusing on irrelevant activities is not a great way to achieve success.

You can spend your time either wisely or foolishly. The degree to which you handle time will determine how much you minimize the conflict between your work life and your personal life. Essential to handling time is developing your ability to focus on the projects that make you the real money and the leisure activities that give you the most satisfaction.

The tendency in corporate life, as in life in general, is to complicate matters. People engage in a myriad of activities that are not only time consuming, but also totally useless. Bizarrely, Workaholics feel important if they have worked long and hard on unproductive projects.

One of the best ways to complicate your existence is to allow yourself to be intimidated by people who use the slogan, "Anything worth doing is worth doing well." If you believe this nonsense, you've struck out even before you've stepped out of the dugout on the way to the batter's box. You will end up investing an inordinate amount of time, emotional energy, and money in things that bring no real return to you.

FOR THE TRULY LAZY:

When you need something tedious done, and don't have time for it, give it to a Workaholic.

This way, both of you will be happy.

More Wisdom for Being a Creative Lazy Achiever:

A lazy person gives the workaholic something worthwhile to do and someone to feel happily superior to.
— JULIA SWIGGUM

I made up my mind long ago that life was too short to do anything for myself that I could pay others to do for me.
— W. SOMERSET MAUGHAM

The most successful people are not workaholics. What they're good at is achieving the best possible results in the shortest period of time.
— ROBERT J. RINGER

Doing the wrong things very well won't get you much success in life. If the key ingredient of your business is telephoning your clients, for example, then you should concentrate most of your efforts on this activity. Spending six hours cleaning your desk and five minutes making phone calls won't be one-tenth as productive as spending one hour on phone calls and five minutes on desk cleaning. In the less productive case, you will have worked six hours and five minutes, whereas you will have worked only one hour and five minutes in the much more productive case.

Chapter 1 stressed the importance of doing your best in the time you have available, but this advice comes with a qualification: the key is to do your best at the important things and to do far from your best at the unimportant things. People who learn to strive for excellence in a few really important areas, instead of striving for a great performance in everything they undertake, are able to turn their lives around 180 degrees.

Again, the key is paying attention. Refuse to get sidetracked by low-priority projects. Just the fact that something is interesting doesn't mean that pursuing it is worthwhile. Even if the activity is helpful, this still doesn't necessarily make doing it worthwhile. The question is, How much does it help? In other words, Is it more helpful than other worthwhile projects you could be actively pursuing?

In fact, you may want to go one step further and ask yourself whether the project has to be done at all. Surprisingly, many people focus on work projects and other activities that bring them absolutely no return in satisfaction and happiness. It doesn't matter if you are active but don't know the true purpose of your activity. Whenever you are working on the wrong things, no matter how much you work, you will never do enough.

FOR THE TRULY LAZY:

THREE WAYS TO HANDLE A TASK FAST

Do it yourself.

Hire an expert to handle it for you.

Decide that it isn't worth doing and strike it off your to-do list.

More Wisdom for Being a Creative Lazy Achiever:

Always do one thing less than you think you can do.
— *BERNARD BARUCH*

Hands down, the fastest way to complete any task is to simply cross it off your To-Do list.
— *ROBERT J. RINGER*

Chuck your to-do list; make a not-to-do list, instead.
— *RICHARD KOCH*

ALL THINGS WORTH DOING WELL AREN'T WORTH OVERDOING

To be successful, you must concentrate on the important things. Still, caution is urged. Not only are most worthwhile things not worth doing well, but all things worth doing well aren't worth overdoing. This is no different than cooking a fine meal. Important work shouldn't be underdone, but neither should it be overdone.

Perfection and excellence are very different things. Doing things in excellence means doing your best with the time, energy, and other resources you have available. This leads to quality results achieved through effective and efficient use of limited resources. On the other hand, doing things with perfection in mind involves trying to achieve what can't be done. It invariably leads to the inefficient and ineffective use of limited resources. Moreover, the results are often dubious at best.

Let me share a personal example: When I started writing my signature book *The Joy of Not Working* on January 1, 1991, I allowed myself until July 31 to complete the first draft. After I beat my deadline by one day, I allowed another month in which to have several friends review the manuscript to suggest changes. Because the software program didn't have a spellcheck, I realized that I wouldn't be aware of all the spelling and grammatical errors even with my volunteer editors helping me.

After making all the changes within the available time, I got my self-published book to the printer and had it published by September 15. By keeping to my to-printer deadline, I was able to introduce the book to the bookstore market well in advance of the competition. Other publishers may have had their books closer to perfection, but I was able to get more and better publicity for my book before the all-important Christmas shopping season, in large part because it was published sooner.

After *The Joy of Not Working* had sold over 30,000 copies, making it a Canadian best-seller for three straight years, I decided to update the book. This time, I used an updated version of the word processing program, which now

FOR THE TRULY LAZY:

To attempt too many things at once is to end up completing none.

Instead of putting mediocre effort into a lot of things, place excellent effort into a few significant things.

One important project carried to home plate will always feel much more satisfying than three projects remaining on first, second, and third.

More Wisdom for Being a Creative Lazy Achiever:

The shortest way to do many things is to do only one thing at once.
— SAMUEL SMILES

Think of many things to do — do one.
— PORTUGUESE PROVERB

had a spellcheck. Surprise! The original edition of the book had 150 spelling errors in it. Did this hurt sales? As near as I can tell, not at all. Although I had one letter from an irate schoolteacher about the number of spelling errors, more than 99 percent of the six hundred-plus letters I received about the book were positive, with no mention of the spelling errors.

The point is, if I had wanted to get everything in the book perfect, I would still be working on it. On the other hand, preparing the book in excellence, even though things were far from perfect, allowed me to bring out a book that has provided me with a nice income for over twenty-seven years. Indeed, it has now sold 310,000 copies and has earned me over $850,000 in pretax profits.

It may come as a surprise to many, but pursuing perfection on important projects is just as harmful as settling for mediocrity. Both lead to dissatisfaction, unhappiness, and a lack of success. "A lot of disappointed people," stated Donald Kennedy, "have been left standing on the street corner waiting for the bus marked 'Perfection.' "

Norman Cousins also put perfection in its place when he declared, "The essence of man is imperfection." Perfection exists not in reality, but only in people's expectations. Like security, perfection is an illusion. Doing anything flawlessly is impossible. Remember that no perfectly published book, no perfectly prepared meal, no perfectly written report, and no perfectly satisfied customer exist.

Like everyone else in this world, you may at times get bitten by the perfection bug. You should resist the urge to attain perfection in any area of your life just as you should resist the urge to be only mediocre in something important to you. You shouldn't end up feeling as though you failed to get things right or fell short of what others might accomplish. Clearly, you don't have to do anything flawlessly to feel successful.

The key is to strive for excellence, which is somewhere between mediocrity and perfection. You must decide where excellence falls. Loosely stated, excellence is putting in the best effort you can given the circumstances and resources. You should do the best you can — but remember, only on the important matters.

FOR THE TRULY LAZY:

If excellence is your theme, then let moderation be your song.

There is no perfect way to complete any project.

Therefore, stop trying to find one.

Whatever is worth doing well is definitely not worth overdoing.

More Wisdom for Being a Creative Lazy Achiever:

Perfection is an elusive butterfly. When we cease to demand perfection, the business of being happy becomes much easier.
— HELEN KELLER

Housework can kill you if done right.
— ERMA BOMBECK

YOUR MOST POWERFUL SUCCESS TOOL

If anything can help you get your life in proper balance, it's the 80-20 rule, first discovered by Italian economist Vilfredo Pareto more than one hundred years ago. Following this rule is incredibly powerful for dealing with a time crunch and avoiding the workaholism that has afflicted much of the Western world. In fact, I have adopted this rule so that I can work four to five hours each day, have a leisurely lifestyle, and still earn a decent income.

Generally speaking, the 80-20 rule states that the first 80 percent of our productivity comes from the first 20 percent of our time and effort. This leaves only 20 percent of our productivity to be attained from the remaining 80 percent of our time and effort. Eighty percent of our time and effort therefore results in relatively insignificant return.

Perhaps you have read one or more of the hundreds of articles written about the 80-20 rule, but like many people who know about it, you don't fully use it for its remarkable potential. Most people who have heard of this principle don't give it more than a passing thought as they waste away their lives. Yet the 80-20 rule can help individuals and corporations achieve greater results using less time, money, and effort.

The 80-20 rule supports the main premise of this book: for more success in your life, try working less but thinking more than does the average person in society. Without doubt, 80-20 thinking can help you achieve much more with much less effort. You can work less, earn more money, and enjoy your personal life like never before. As a bonus, following the 80-20 rule day in and day out can make you wealthy over the long term.

Perhaps you are wondering, If the 80-20 rule is so effective, why doesn't everyone use it? The answer, quite simply, is that it requires creative thinking, and it requires being different and unconventional. These two requirements keep the majority of people from using it.

Albert Schweitzer advised, "Think first, then do." Many people get frantically involved in a lot of activities without ever getting around to thinking

FOR THE TRULY LAZY:

Never lose sight of the 80-20 rule:

The first 80 percent of your results come from the first 20 percent of your time and effort and the remaining 20 percent of your results require a whopping 80 percent of your time and effort.

Be willing to do without the last 20 percent of results if they aren't that important.

Apply this rule not just in your work, but in your personal life as well, and you will have mastered being a lazy but highly intelligent and productive human being.

More Wisdom for Being a Creative Lazy Achiever:

Laziness is nothing to be ashamed of. It's just efficiency, the proper use of resources.

— JULIA SWIGGUM

why they are involved in them. Consequently, they spend most of their efforts on unproductive activities. It shouldn't be a surprise that they are continually stressed out and time-deprived.

The power to decide what activities are important and the commitment to focus on those activities are basic to having a balanced lifestyle. "Things that matter most," said Goethe, "must never be at the mercy of things that matter least." Clearly, most of what we do in life has little value when it comes to our happiness and satisfaction.

Given the high probability that you spend 80 percent of your time on low priority activities, you must reassess how much time you want to spend on these activities. To make the optimum use of your time, you must get rid of the 80 percent of activities that give you only 20 percent of your results. You may not be able to do away with all of these activities, but you can do away with many of them. If you can eliminate at least half of your low-value activities, you will open up an abundance of time for pursuing leisure in your life.

You may claim that you cannot eliminate any of your low-value activities. This is hogwash. Although you may perceive all activities as necessary ingredients for performing your work efficiently, most are not.

Practically everyone has at least some latitude for eliminating low-result activities. No one operates at peak efficiency. Eliminating low-result activities can be difficult from an emotional perspective but is possible if you set your mind to it. At work, you may have to give up your obsession with perfection in everything you undertake. You may also have to give up pet projects that offer little value toward the results you hope to attain.

Learn to identify where you get a lot more than you put in. Also identify the areas where you get back a fraction of what you put in. The objective is to maximize results from the areas of great surpluses and to bail out of those activities with big deficits.

Especially if you are self-employed or own a business, the 80-20 rule allows you to earn more and work less by choosing the right things to do and doing only those things that add the highest value to your income. You will find that you need not have a shortage of time to devote to your personal life.

FOR THE TRULY LAZY:

Be creative as well as selective.

Placing outstanding creative effort into two or three important things will make you much more successful than putting average effort into many things.

More Wisdom for Being a Creative Lazy Achiever:

What I do, I do very well, and what I don't do well, I don't do at all.
— UNKNOWN WISE PERSON

It's the freest feeling in the world to rid yourself of projects and activities that clutter your life and contribute little or nothing to the achievement of your goals. You should be spending most of your time concentrating on constructive projects and activities that have the potential to make a real difference in the quality of your life.
— ROBERT J. RINGER

Even if you work for a corporation, adopting the 80-20 rule will help you to produce two or three times as much as the average person produces in a normal workday. Sooner or later, good management will reward you, and your income will reflect your productivity. Having an optimum work-life balance should be a cinch if you limit yourself to working regular hours.

For your life to work, and work well, you must apply the 80-20 rule ruthlessly to all areas of life. You must eliminate unnecessary activities that offer little benefit to your income, happiness, or satisfaction. Contrary to what society believes, the key to a fulfilling life is to work as hard as you have to for a comfortable living and as little as you can get away with. The 80-20 rule allows you to do this.

With the 80-20 rule as your most powerful tool, you can take creative liberties to live the way you would like to live instead of the way the masses do. Not only will you create an excellent life-work balance, but you will find that work is much more pleasurable and satisfying — especially when you can produce a lot more results and money with a lot less effort and time.

SLOW DOWN AND YOUR DAYS WILL BE LONGER

Time is supposed to be money. In fact, time is worth more than money. If you lose money, you can replace it with much more money. Doing the same with time is impossible. As Benjamin Franklin declared, "Lost time is never found again." In this regard, money is unlimited; time isn't. Unfortunately, some people act as if the opposite were true.

Clearly, in today's fast-paced, stressed-out Western world, time is at a premium as never before. Time is, in fact, our scarcest resource. It is a finite resource on which we place infinite demands by trying to do too much. Given that you can always get more money but not more time, you should spend your time much more wisely than you spend your money.

Billionaire Nicolas Hayek, who reshaped the insolvent Swiss watch industry into a multibillion-dollar empire, had this to say about time: "Time is both wonderful and horrible. It is my work and life. Yet I hate time. Why?

FOR THE TRULY LAZY:

Remember to exploit the 80-20 rule to its fullest.

Always act 80-20; think 80-20; work 80-20; and play 80-20.

No special talent is required.

Just pay close attention to whatever you are doing in life.

More Wisdom for Being a Creative Lazy Achiever:

It is the superfluous things for which men sweat.
— *SENECA*

Most of the critical things in life, which become the starting points for human destiny, are little things.
— *R. SMITH*

Because you cannot stop it. You cannot possess it. It's always present, but if you try to hold it, it disappears. And don't try to use personal tricks to fool time. It will always catch up with you."

Your mind is your greatest asset, but it can play tricks on you. One such nasty trick is that it makes you believe that you don't have sufficient time to do your work and still have a satisfying, balanced lifestyle with time for relaxation, social engagements, and other leisure activities. Perhaps you should think again! You have 1,440 minutes, or 86,400 seconds, in a day. That's the same amount of time that everyone else on this Earth has, including people who have a full, relaxed, happy, and satisfying lifestyle.

Putting more time into your life is actually quite easy. Whenever you are short on time for the good things in life, you must create more time by making better use of what you have. A recent research study at Penn State University indicated that what we see as a time crunch is in large measure just an erroneous perception. We all have enough time to do the important and enjoyable things, but we squander it. If we make excellent use of just 30 or 40 percent of our time, we shouldn't have any shortage.

It may appear that the way to put more time in your life is to rush more during the day and try to do as many things as possible in the shortest time. Perhaps you have tried this many times and discovered that you always feel even more time-deprived. No wonder that an old Dutch saying contends, "The hurrier we go, the behinder we get."

To be sure, squeezing as many leisure activities as possible into your personal time won't help you attain a balanced and relaxed lifestyle. Ironically, the activities that are supposed to help you relieve stress and enhance your health can actually have the reverse effect if you try to rush through them. Exercising in a hurry, for example, is liable to create more stress than it dissipates. In the same vein, you can't meditate effectively if you feel rushed. You are likely to regret having meditated at all when you realize that you have wasted your time.

In the corporate environment, time management is frequently touted as a tool for controlling time and putting more time into our lives. Time

FOR THE TRULY LAZY:

You can't earn more time, no matter how hard you work.

And you can't buy it, no matter how much money you have.

So spend it wisely, much more so than money.

More Wisdom for Being a Creative Lazy Achiever:

A day is a span of time no one is wealthy enough to waste.
— UNKNOWN WISE PERSON

I were better to be eaten to death with a rust than to be scoured to nothing with perpetual motion.
— WILLIAM SHAKESPEARE

Things that matter most must never be at the mercy of things that matter least.
— JOHANN WOLFGANG VON GOETHE

management isn't as effective as most people think, however, because it supports trying to do more and more in a limited amount of time. The problem with using time management techniques is that you still dedicate a lot of your effort and time to things that are unimportant.

Instead of *managing time*, you must *transcend* time. Part of the total experience of being a Creative Lazy Achiever is being able to do your own thing at your own speed. Again, forget about what the masses are doing. Even if practically everyone else seems to increase the pace of life every day, you don't have to try to keep up. You must take control of your physical and psychic space instead of allowing the distractions of the modern world to influence your lifestyle.

The Creative Lazy Achiever's secret to mastering time may surprise you: to make your days longer, don't rush; slow down instead. In a somewhat magical way, you will have more time when you start living every moment for all it is worth. Once you slow down, you will no longer fight time; you will master it. Full involvement and appreciation of any activity, whether writing your first novel, walking in the park, talking to your neighbor, or taking a shower, will make the whole world slow down for you.

The next time you think that you don't have time to enjoy a sunset, think about it a little more. You will realize that the most important time to enjoy a sunset is when you don't have time for it. Taking ten minutes to watch the sun go down will do more to help you catch up with the world than rushing around for several hours. To your surprise, the world will actually slow down for you.

The more sunsets you stop to enjoy, the more relaxed and less rushed life will be. Moreover, you will realize the importance of utilizing the 80-20 rule to reduce the quantity of your other activities so that you get more quality from what you do pursue. You need not apologize to anyone for slowing down and enjoying life. Not everyone will approve of your behavior, but this adds to your personal satisfaction.

FOR THE TRULY LAZY:

Away from work, do the simple things that are important for your happiness.

Spend time with the people you like the most.

Get involved in the activities that you enjoy most.

And totally avoid the people and activities that you like least.

Indeed, this strategy is so obvious, but few people use it.

More Wisdom for Being a Creative Lazy Achiever:

Time is what we want most, but . . . what we use worst.
— *WILLIAM PENN*

Well-arranged time is the surest mark of a well-arranged mind.
— *SIR ISAAC PITMAN*

Chapter 6

The Journey

TOWARD SUCCESS

Should Feel Better than

THE ARRIVAL

FOR THE TRULY LAZY:

This cannot be emphasized enough:

Choose your activities wisely.

Spend your time and energy on the important few instead of on the insignificant many.

Once you have this mastered, you will achieve success and happiness beyond your wildest dreams.

More Wisdom for Being a Creative Lazy Achiever:

Does it matter? If so, how much does it matter?
— *ROBERT J. RINGER*

Nothing matters very much, and few things matter at all.
— *EARL BALFOUR*

ONLY FOOLS ARE IN A HURRY TO GET TO ANYWHERE WORTH GOING

Perhaps you would like to amass a pile of money that would make Bill Gates or Oprah Winfrey look like paupers. Alternatively, you may be after the Pulitzer, the Nobel, an Oscar, a Tony, a Juno, or an Emmy. There is nothing wrong with getting your name in bright lights, but rest assured that it won't happen overnight. Nor will it happen in a year or two. In fact, it may never happen if you don't relax and take your time while striving to get to where you want to go.

Contrary to popular belief, life isn't all about attaining as much fame and fortune as possible, in the shortest possible time, without any regard to how it's made. Yet the popularity of ABC TV's quiz show *Who Wants to Be a Millionaire?* indicated that many people aspire to fame and fortune now instead of later, without regard to how they get there. "Fast, with minimum effort," has become the preferred mode for success.

In the modern world, people are easily caught up in the mania of fast and easy success, especially if they believe that all individuals who attain fame and fortune through their creative efforts do so overnight. Immediate gratification is the driving force that has people looking for a fast track to fame and fortune. Unfortunately, immediate gratification is one of the most expensive needs exhibited by humans. Not only does striving for such gratification often lead to bankruptcy court, it often delays — or even prevents the attainment of success.

Like many people in Western society, you may dream of getting rich quickly so that you can quit your job and start enjoying life for all it's worth. Pressure to make a quick fortune isn't conducive to your present-day physical and emotional health, however. Constant pressure will also negatively affect your financial and personal well-being, especially if you lose your health.

The wise people in this world tell us that only fools are in a hurry to get to anywhere worth going. Regardless of what we are trying to accomplish, we will do ourselves great good to remember the words of Thomas Shadwell: "The haste of a fool is the slowest thing in the world." Rushing about in desperation

FOR THE TRULY LAZY:

Do you often find yourself in a hurry to attain personal success?

If so, since when was anything of value created suddenly?

More Wisdom for Being a Creative Lazy Achiever:

Going faster doesn't give us more time — it makes us feel that we're always behind.
— RICHARD KOCH

Wisely and slowly. They stumble that run fast.
— WILLIAM SHAKESPEARE

No man who is in a hurry is quite civilized.
— WILL DURANT

The last thing in the world you want to do is mistake speed for direction, because if your emphasis is on speed alone, you could be moving sideways. Worse, you could be moving backward.
— ROBERT J. RINGER

will only push what we are really after — satisfaction, health, peace of mind, and happiness — away from us.

True success, which contributes to satisfaction, peace of mind, and happiness, requires action, but also patience. Impatient people seldom arrive where they are going — and if they do, it normally takes them much longer to get there than it takes patient people.

Focusing on success itself, instead of on the process by which you earn it, isn't the surest way to attain it. The following ancient poem by Chang Tzu warns of the dangers of focusing on the prize instead of on the process.

THE NEED TO WIN

When an archer is shooting for nothing
He has all his skill
If he shoots for a brass buckle
He is already nervous
If he shoots for a prize of gold
He goes blind
Or sees two targets
He is out of his mind!
His skill has not changed. But the prize
Divides him. He cares
He thinks more of winning
Than of shooting —
And the need to win
Drains him of power.

As a Creative Lazy Achiever, you don't have to race toward the attainment of success. What seems urgent seldom is. By slowing down, you will be able to tap your creativity and come up with ideas that can make a difference in the lives of others, and to the world as a whole. This will put you in a position to implement your ideas and create abundant wealth in the long term. Paradoxically, when you become less preoccupied with attaining success itself and with attaining it in a hurry, success comes easier and quicker.

FOR THE TRULY LAZY:

RULE NO. 1

It's foolish to be in a hurry to acquire the insignificant things in life.

This leaves the significant things to rush after.

RULE NO. 2

If you hurry to acquire the significant things in life, you will take longer to acquire them than if you do not hurry.

More Wisdom for Being a Creative Lazy Achiever:

Does thou love life? Then do not squander time, for that's the stuff life is made of.
— BENJAMIN FRANKLIN

There is no greatness where there is not simplicity.
— LEO TOLSTOY

The most important thing is not the prize, but the journey and your commitment to enjoy the journey. Have some fun and adventure along the way. If you slow down and tap into your imagination, you will come up with money-making projects that people in a hurry to get rich never see. Not being in a hurry also means having the time to observe what's happening around you in the present moment. That's where life is — and always will be.

When you choose to be a Creative Lazy Achiever, you choose to be the smart tortoise instead of the foolish hare. The foolish hare rushes around trying to accumulate as much fame and fortune as possible. In a mad frenzy, the hare tries to get to that destination called happiness.

On the other hand, the tortoise doesn't have to try to accumulate as much stuff and recognition as the hare, knowing full well that those things won't make it happy. The smart tortoise doesn't hurry, because it's already arrived at that destination called happiness: it's experiencing peace and satisfaction from what it presently has.

LIFE'S A BREEZE WHEN WE PUT HALF AS MUCH TIME INTO SIMPLIFYING IT AS WE DO INTO COMPLICATING IT

Life is obviously a lot easier when we keep things simple. Unfortunately, given a choice between a simple way and a difficult way of doing things, most of us choose the difficult one. Preposterous as it may seem, some of us even spend time inventing a difficult way when none is immediately available.

We do not need to make our lives more difficult. Given the opportunity, plenty of other individuals in this world will gladly do this for us. Life's unexpected events will also put our creativity to the ultimate test without our having to create our own special difficulties.

Albert Einstein stated, "Everything should be made as simple as possible, but not simpler." We need not worry about people making things too simple in their lives. On the contrary — most people make their lives too complicated and wonder why they have so many big headaches and major problems.

FOR THE TRULY LAZY:

M ost people complicate their lives more than they care to admit.

K eep in mind that all it takes is a muddlehead to make the simple complicated.

I t takes a genius to make the complicated simple, however.

T he choice is yours: muddlehead or genius?

More Wisdom for Being a Creative Lazy Achiever:

I adore simple pleasures. They are the last refuge of the complex.
— OSCAR WILDE

We struggle with the complexities and avoid the simplicities.
— NORMAN VINCENT PEALE

Do not embrace what you don't want. You are liable to get it.
— LIFE'S SECRET HANDBOOK

Why people make their lives unnecessarily difficult is a mystery to philosophers and psychiatrists alike. I am just as amazed at how far most people will go to find the myriad of methods to complicate their personal and business lives. They waste a lot of money, time, and energy on pursuing things that bring them nothing in return. They hang around people who do them absolutely no good. Perhaps many if not most humans are masochists.

At some point, most of us tend to make our lives difficult and complicated. We come close to being buried alive in our junk and clutter. We do this with our possessions, work-related activities, relationships, family affairs, thoughts, and emotions. We are unable to achieve as much as we would like because we invite too many distractions into our lives. Indeed, life is easy when we put half as much time into simplifying it as we do into complicating it.

If you are the type of person who can't leave home without four-fifths of your personal possessions, it's time to lighten up a little on your journey through life. Without delay, get rid of the burdens that have drained your time, space, money, and energy. Do something today to make your life less complicated. Refuse to spend time with people or things that are irrelevant to leading a fulfilled life, for example.

As a Creative Lazy Achiever enjoying life to its fullest, identify regularly what no longer adds to a relaxed lifestyle. Apply the 80-20 rule to both personal and career aspects of your life. Make a list of the things that no longer serve a worthwhile purpose in your world. Ask your friends to add to this list with suggestions as to how you can simplify things. Your friends may see some opportunity where you see none.

The Roman philosopher Seneca stated, "No man can swim ashore and take his baggage with him." Whatever your destination, you can't afford to carry excess baggage. On trains and airlines, excess baggage will cost you extra money. On the trip called life, excess baggage will cost you much more than money. At best, you won't succeed in achieving your goals as quickly as you otherwise could. At worst, you will never succeed in attaining your goals. Not only will this deprive you of satisfaction and happiness, but it could cost you your sanity in the end.

FOR THE TRULY LAZY:

Identify the important.

Also identify the unimportant.

Then filter out the unimportant, and concentrate on the important.

You are now on your way to all the success you need in life.

More Wisdom for Being a Creative Lazy Achiever:

If your mind isn't clouded by unnecessary things, this is the best season of your life.
— *WU-MEN*

The ability to simplify means to eliminate the unnecessary so that the necessary may speak.
— *HANS HOFMANN*

ENVY IS THE SATISFACTION AND HAPPINESS THAT WE THINK OTHERS ARE EXPERIENCING

Economists say that all of us have insatiable wants. If this were the case, no one should be able to attain happiness. Many individuals, including Creative Lazy Achievers, are nonetheless happy. Clearly, happiness can be attained in this world without all of our unlimited wants being satisfied.

For most of us, the ideal life is the life we do not lead, the life that someone else leads. In this regard, a French proverb proclaims, "What you can't get is just what suits you."

What makes many of us unhappy, to the point of extreme misery, is our unreasonable and false beliefs about how happy others are. We have some strange idea that most people in Western society are happier than we are. Yet this is far from being the case. As Joseph Roux surmised, "I look at what I have not and think myself unhappy; others look at what I have and think me happy."

It's easy to fall into the trap of thinking that practically everyone else has a much easier and happier life than you do. There will always be friends, relatives, neighbors, or celebrities who own bigger houses, drive flashier cars, wear more expensive clothes, work at better jobs, or have more physically attractive lovers. How happy they are is another matter. If they are envious of people who have things that they do not have, they certainly aren't happy.

One of the most important factors for enjoying life to the fullest is an absence of envy for others. Envy, in fact, is the satisfaction and happiness that we think others are experiencing but aren't. Many, perhaps most, of the individuals we envy aren't any happier than we are. Even many of the rich and famous don't make good targets for our envy. Singer and actress Barbra Streisand warned us, "Oh God, don't envy me, I have my own pains."

To envy the rich and famous is rather ill-considered in light of the fact that many of these individuals aren't happy. If you are going to envy anyone, envy the poor of this world who are happy. Being happy takes some inspirational doing on their part.

FOR THE TRULY LAZY:

Be careful with success.

It's best to stop and ponder what it all means once you acquire it.

Success can also cause misery and dejection.

Don't be surprised when you learn it doesn't bring you all the happiness and peace of mind you thought it would.

More Wisdom for Being a Creative Lazy Achiever:

Nothing is so good as it seems beforehand.
— GEORGE ELIOT

Life is so constructed that the event does not, cannot, will not, match the expectation.
— CHARLOTTE BRONTE

Another important point is that experiencing envy has practically no benefit. Envy is an extremely heavy burden to carry because it breeds contempt and hatred. Someone once said, "Envy is like acid; it eats away the container that it's in."

No matter how hard you try, you can't be both envious and happy. Envy and unhappiness go hand in hand. Envy of even one person is a mistake. What's the point of admiring someone else's fortunes so much that you become dissatisfied with your own? Comparing your position with that of others can lead to disillusionment and frustration. You will end up unfairly thinking well of others and disliking yourself.

While you are playing the comparison game, why not play it both ways? Perhaps you would like to live in one of twenty countries, such as Sierra Leone or Afghanistan, where rampant poverty, lack of health care, serious malnutrition, constant violence, and perpetual crime contribute to a life expectancy of less than forty-eight years.

The way to overcome envy of others is to relax and count your blessings more often. At least once a week, think about the great things your country offers that other countries don't. When you feel deprived because someone has something you don't, keep in mind that billions of people in other countries would gladly trade places with you.

Gratitude for what you have will do wonders for your well-being. "Just think how happy you would be," an unknown wise person declared, "if you lost everything you have right now, and then got it back." When you regularly take the time to appreciate the things you have — your health, your home, your friends, your music collection, your knowledge, and your creative ability — you won't have time to be envious of others.

To be happy, you must be grateful for many things in life — and there are many if you really look. To identify more of the things for which you should be grateful, borrow an idea from Oprah Winfrey: Keep a gratitude journal. At the end of every day, count your blessings and write down at least five wonderful things that happened to you that day. In no time, envy will be a thing of the past, and happiness will flow naturally.

FOR THE TRULY LAZY:

Understand that the success you have at any moment is the only success you can ever experience.

Reminisce about your great yesterdays, hope for many interesting tomorrows, but, above all, ensure that you live today.

More Wisdom for Being a Creative Lazy Achiever:

The power for creating a better future is contained in the present moment: You create a good future by creating a good present.
— *ECKHART TOLLE*

Taking full advantage of the present to live the moment and at the same time make a big difference in this world is undeniable proof of your agreement to live your life now — while you have it — and be dead later — when you are.
— *LIFE'S SECRET HANDBOOK*

Infinite patience leads to immediate results.
— *A COURSE IN MIRACLES*

BE HAPPY WHILE YOU ARE ALIVE,
BECAUSE YOU ARE A LONG TIME DEAD

A *Globe and Mail* article a while ago cited Richard Israels of Vancouver, who died of colon cancer at the age of fifty-one. Not even in the last few months of his life did Israels lament over his unfortunate affliction. Because of his zest and exuberance, his relatively short life had been exciting and satisfying. He reflected just before his death, "No matter what, I had a good run."

Making "a good run" at life requires that we pursue what is most important to us. A full, relaxed, happy, and satisfying life isn't determined so much by how long we live as by how well we live. Some people die at forty-five, but they squeeze in a lot more real living than do others who live to be ninety-five or a hundred.

If your life is a good case study in perpetual stress and turmoil, there's no point in declaring, "I may not be here for a good time, but at least I'm here for a long time!" What's the point of being here for a long time if you don't enjoy yourself? Besides, you won't have to worry about what to do in retirement if your whole life is in crisis when you are still young. Death will preclude even an early retirement.

Henry David Thoreau warned, "Oh, God, to reach the point of death and realize you have never lived at all." Most people over sixty-five sooner or later look back on their lives with regret. They feel sorry they didn't set their priorities differently. Most wish that they hadn't been so concerned about the little things and had spent more time doing the things they wanted to do.

Assume that you wind up on your death bed in the next month. You say to God, "Please, give me one more shot, and I will give it all I've got." God replies, "Okay. You can have one more year of healthy living for doing what you have always wanted to do."

The million-dollar question is, What would you do in the last year? Making a list of the activities that you would pursue is a worthwhile exercise. Put the completed list in your wallet, and carry it with you at all times to remind

FOR THE TRULY LAZY:

L ive a little.

L augh a little.

L ove a little.

H appiness will find you in a big way.

More Wisdom for Being a Creative Lazy Achiever:

Play a happy tune and happy dancers will join your trip.
— THADDEUS GOLAS

Living just to get by is not enough. Just like the butterfly, an adventurous soul needs a varied and enchanting life — green grass and happy skies, freedom to go where it pleases, and joys that await it.
— LIFE'S SECRET HANDBOOK

yourself of what is important to you. Instead of risking later regret that you have not pursued the important things in life, take the time to pursue most of them now.

In truth, the best way to achieve long-term happiness is to experience perpetual short-term happiness. It's important to have a good balance between work and play in the present. Putting off a happy work-life balance until years down the road is tantamount to putting off sex until after you retire from your job. In either case, it ain't gonna work.

It's also important to quit worrying about what the future will bring. If you want the future to be better than the present, you must live mostly in the present instead of in the future. Stop to enjoy what you already have but haven't been enjoying. Take stock of the valuables, treasures, and talents that you have misplaced, lost, or forgotten in your hurried lifestyle — good books, true friendships, artistic pursuits, hobbies, passions, and personal dreams.

You will have many days when career, financial, or personal matters aren't as bright as you would like them to be. Nevertheless, you need not whine that your life isn't as good as it could be. Doing so will only distract you from all the good things happening in your life. You may even miss out completely on these important experiences.

Rather than focusing on what's wrong with the world, focus on what's right. If you generally insist on criticizing and complaining, try spending four times as much time praising the good things and expressing gratitude as you do criticizing and complaining. This is as it should be; studies show that 80 percent of the events in our lives are positive and 20 percent negative.

Make every attempt to avoid sacrificing today's well-being for money and the material things that you believe will bring you future happiness. Think about it. By the time you acquire these things, it may be too late for you to enjoy them. You may never in the future have the health to enjoy these things. Moreover, even if you do, you will likely discover that these things don't bring happiness as you originally thought they would.

Take a close look at the great people of the world, such as Mother Teresa, the Dalai Lama, Nelson Mandela, and Mahatma Gandhi. These remarkable

FOR THE TRULY LAZY:

L ook at the world around you.

I t may seem like a hard place to live, and a harder place to be happy.

I t is neither.

W ith the right attitude — and a moderate amount of creative effort — you can make it a paradise unto itself.

More Wisdom for Being a Creative Lazy Achiever:

Be content with what you have; rejoice in the way things are. When you realize there is nothing lacking, the whole world belongs to you.
— TAO TE CHING

One day you will wake up and there won't be any more time to do the things you've always wanted. Do it now.
— PAULO COELHO

individuals lived or live with little but have experienced happiness, joy, and self-fulfillment throughout their lives. They didn't pursue happiness and self-fulfillment as goals in themselves. Happiness and self-fulfillment resulted from a much higher purpose — a purpose that involved working toward the common good of humanity.

Few of us derive our greatest joys in life from money, power, or prestige. Joy comes from the satisfaction of total immersion in doing something worthwhile. Instead of money, or something derived from it, a worthwhile activity — either work related or leisure related — becomes its own reward.

It doesn't matter so much what you do for a living, or how much fame and fortune you attain, as whether you enjoy peace, health, and love while you do it. If you don't have these, what can replace them? Don't lose sight of the fact that happiness is not a destination but a journey, a by-product of performing a job well, having good health, doing our duty, pursuing our goals, accepting the inevitable, loving the world, showing gratitude, helping other individuals to be happy, and living fully.

Your goal should be to make your stay on Earth as close to a Heavenly experience as it can be. Indeed, Zen masters tell us that there is no sense in waiting for Heaven. Zen says that this is life, and today, this is Heaven.

Put another way, this is it! Today, this is all you get. Take it or leave it. And you can't leave it. Therefore, make the best of it. This way, in the event you get to Heaven, you will be well prepared to enjoy yourself there.

The rest of your life begins right now. It can be more than it has ever been. Your goal should be to enjoy everything in life that you can. It is a mistake not to. Let it be a wondrous life. Life is all around you. Live it to its fullest, with all your senses. Listen to it. Look at it. Taste it. Smell it. Feel it.

By all means, spend a good part of your life attaining the personal success that you would like to attain. Ensure, however, that you, like the Costa Rican fisherman, have a full, relaxed, satisfying, and happy life along the way. Whatever success means to you, your journey toward it should feel better than your arrival. If you are doing what's right for you, it will.

FOR THE TRULY LAZY:

As a Creative Lazy Achiever you can make a big difference in this world.

As big of a difference as the hardest workers of this world will make, in fact.

No doubt you will find an easier and happier way to do so.

And with much more Swagger, too!

More Wisdom for Being a Creative Lazy Achiever:

Swagger is the natural companion of creative laziness.
— BENJAMIN A. SLOAN

There's no point in success if you don't let it go to your head. That's what it's for.
— JOHN OTWAY

Don't ever grow up. Be forever young in spirit. Spend your entire life in the most inspirational, adventurous, and creative way possible.
— LIFE'S SECRET HANDBOOK

About the Author

Ernie J. Zelinski is an international best-selling author, professional speaker, unconventional career expert, and prosperity life coach who inspires adventurous souls to live prosperous and free. Ernie's core message — that ordinary people can attain out-of-the-ordinary results and make a difference in this world — is at the heart of his work.

Ernie is the author of the international bestsellers *How to Retire Happy, Wild, and Free* (over 400,000 copies sold and published in 11 languages), and *The Joy of Not Working* (over 310,000 copies sold and published in 17 foreign languages), two life-changing books that have helped hundreds of thousands of individuals around the world live happier and more satisfying lives.

Ernie's creative works have now sold over 1,000,000 copies worldwide. Feature articles about Ernie and his books have appeared in major newspapers including *USA TODAY*, *Oakland Tribune*, *Boston Herald*, *The Washington Post*, and *Toronto Star*.

Ernie's latest books include the inspirational novel *Look Ma, Life's Easy: How Ordinary People Attain Extraordinary Success and Remarkable Prosperity* and its companion *Life's Secret Handbook: Reminders for Adventurous Souls Who Want to Make a Big Difference in This World*.

Ernie speaks on the topics of retirement and creativity. He recently made a keynote speech about *The Joy of Not Working* to over 2,000 executives and scholars at the National Turkish Congress on Quality in Istanbul and to 1,200 career experts at the National Career Development Assn. convention in Orlando.

You can contact Ernie about speaking at your important event by emailing him at vipbooks@telus.net or telephoning him at 780-434-9202.

Learn more about Ernie's creative pursuits at:

www.erniezelinski.com

www.retirement-cafe.com

Life-Changing Books by Ernie Zelinski

THE JOY OF NOT WORKING: A Book for the Retired, Unemployed, and Overworked 21st Century Edition

Ernie Zelinski could change your view of the world forever. Ernie has already taught more than 310,000 people what *The Joy of Not Working* is all about: learning to live every part of your life — employment, unemployment, retirement, and leisure time alike — to the fullest. You too can join the thousands of converts and learn to thrive at both work and play. Illustrated by eye-opening exercises, thought-provoking diagrams, and lively cartoons and quotations, *The Joy of Not Working* will guide you to enjoy life like never before.

HOW TO RETIRE HAPPY, WILD, AND FREE: Retirement Wisdom That You Won't Get from Your Financial Advisor

The World's Best Retirement Book is for those individuals who absolutely, positively want to make retirement the best time of their lives. Nancy Conroy of the Association of Pre-Retirement Planners raves: "*How to Retire Happy, Wild, and Free* is optimistic, practical, humorous, and provocative AND comprehensively addresses the many issues impacting individuals as they think about their retirement." *How to Retire Happy, Wild, and Free* has sold over 400,000 copies, and has been published in 11 languages.

Manufactured by Amazon.ca
Bolton, ON

13077764R00141